WHO WILL CARE
FOR US?

WHO WILL CARE FOR US?

Long-Term Care and
the Long-Term Workforce

Paul Osterman

Russell Sage Foundation • **New York**

The Russell Sage Foundation

Library of Congress Cataloging-in-Publication Data

Names: Osterman, Paul, author.
 Title: Who will care for us? : long-term care and the long-term workforce / Paul Osterman.
 Description: New York : Russell Sage Foundation, [2017] | Includes bibliographical references and index.
 Identifiers: LCCN 2017003407 (print) | LCCN 2017021169 (ebook) | ISBN 9781610448673 (ebook) | ISBN 9780871546395 (pbk. : alk. paper)
 Subjects: LCSH: Older people—Care—United States. | Long-term care of the sick—United States. | Home health aides—United States. | Home care services—United States. | Caregivers—United States.
 Classification: LCC HV1461 (ebook) | LCC HV1461 .O77 2017 (print) | DDC 362.160973—dc23
 LC record available at https://lccn.loc.gov/2017003407

Text design by Genna Patacsil.

RUSSELL SAGE FOUNDATION
112 East 64th Street, New York, New York 10065
10 9 8 7 6 5 4 3 2 1

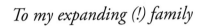

To my expanding (!) family

CONTENTS

LIST OF ILLUSTRATIONS

ABOUT THE AUTHOR

PAUL OSTERMAN is NTU Professor at the Massachusetts Institute of Technology Sloan School of Management.

ACKNOWLEDGMENTS

A great many people helped me with this book, and without their assistance there is no possibility that I could have succeeded. My greatest debts are to Steve Dawson and Carol Rodat, both of PHI, who talked with me numerous times and also provided me with important contacts. Pam Doty of the U.S. Department of Health and Human Services also suffered through repeated conversations and shared a great deal of information.

Several people were remarkably generous with their time and agreed to see me a second or third time. I thank Nancy Hendley, Jim Toews, Bruce Bullen, Alison Barkoff, and Helen Schaub.

Over the course of this book, I interviewed many people. I promised confidentiality to some, particularly direct care workers themselves, and so cannot thank them by name, but I am very appreciative. Other people whom I am very pleased to thank include Kelly Aiken, Gretchen Alkema, Hani Atrash, Nancy Avitabile, Alex Baker, Susan Beane, Adam Berman, Amy J. Berman, Barry Berman, Don Berwick, Patty Blake, Valerie Bogart, Alice Bonner, Linda Bub, Brian Burwell, Harneen Chernow, Maureen Conway, Jeannie Cross, Katie DeAngelis, Barbara Dyer, Susan Eckstein, Corinne Eldridge, Michael Elsas, Alvin Empalmado, Pat Fairchild, Anna Fay, Penny Feldman, Claudia Fine, Len Fishman, Marki Flannery, Laura Fortman, Susan Friedrich, Jacqueline Martinez Garcel, David Gould, Lisa Gurgone, Rebecca Gutman, Andrew Hamilton, Julian Harris, Kathryn Haslanger, Tony Iton, Sheniqua Johnson, Patrick Jordan, Mark Kantor, Manmeet Kaur, Peter Kemper, Mary Jo Kiepper, Jim Knickman, Matt Kudish, Maryjoan Ladden, Joel Lamstein, Joseph W. Larkin, Sarah Leberstein, Don Leopold, Carol

Levine, Wayne Lowell, Audrey Lum, Kevin Mahoney, Cindy Mann, Harry Margolis, Abby Marquand, Jane Martin, Bob Master, Suzanne Modigliani, Jean Moore, Vincent Mor, Bill Moss, Ted Mouw, Al Norman, Michelle Osterman, Michael Piore, Ellen Polivy, Peggy Powell, Charissa Raynor, Jennifer Reckrey, Susan C. Reinhard, Hye Jin Rho, David Rolf, Joe Rosenblom, Helena Ross, Jerry Rubin, Cathy Ruckelshaus, David Russell, Miriam Ryvicker, Francis Sadler, Susan Silbey, June Simmons, Lois Simon, Theresa A. Soriano, Robyn Stone, Tom Strong, Jodi M. Sturgeon, Rick Surpin, Rebecca Sussman, Katherine Swartz, Jay Talbot, Laura Tatum, Harriett Tolpin, Shawna Trager, Hollis Turnham, David Weil, Hannah Weinstock, Joshua Wiener, Patrick Wightman, and Randy Wilson.

I did much of the research for this book while I was a visiting scholar at the Russell Sage Foundation, an opportunity I deeply appreciate. Suzanne Nichols at Russell Sage provided strong support and guidance for this book. Additional financial support was provided by the Smith Richardson Foundation and is much appreciated.

PREFACE

This is a book about long-term care and the challenges we will face as the need for it grows dramatically with the aging of the baby boom generation. Of the many facets to this issue, I focus here on the direct care workers who deliver long-term care and do so by placing their circumstances in the context of the larger long-term care system within which they operate.

Without a direct care workforce, there is no way to meet the looming need, yet today these workers are poorly trained, poorly compensated, disrespected, and restricted in their duties. This state of affairs is problematic for several reasons. First, we will need to attract many more people to the field as demand grows, but today's pay and work conditions make that a hard sell. Second, as the book will show, improving the jobs would improve care and reduce health care costs, neither of which is likely to happen without such improvement. Finally, with no shift in the nature of direct care work, these workers will continue to swell America's large low-wage workforce, and the corrosive inequality that characterizes the job market will become even more entrenched.

There are two fundamental challenges to improving direct care jobs. The first is what might be termed cultural or attitudinal. Many of the key actors in the system have little respect for long-term care workers, and this disrespect is an important obstacle to any effort to improve the job. Other obstacles are more practical: care delivery is so extraordinarily complicated and piecemeal that the term "system" is hardly appropriate, conveying as it does a misleading impression of order and logic. The system's complexity makes any reform difficult to implement. Similarly, financing arrangements are difficult to understand and even harder to align in ways that would lead to reforms. To make matters even worse, the interests of some important actors in the long-term care system occasionally compete with those of long-term care workers or obstruct efforts to improve their jobs.

The objective of this book is to examine these issues and make the case that improving the jobs and circumstances of direct care workers is both desirable and feasible. The book's analysis and argument unfold in three steps. First, I describe the long-term care workforce, detailing who they are, what they do, how they are treated and viewed, and the nature of the labor market within which they operate. Next, I provide evidence of the feasibility of enhancing long-term care workers' skills and expanding their scope of practice, and I argue that doing so will improve care, attract the workforce we need, and reduce system costs. Finally, I describe the considerable obstacles to accomplishing these goals, as well as the reasons to think that they can be overcome.

Importantly, I argue in this book that the challenges of the long-term care workforce cannot be addressed without understanding the larger system in which these workers are embedded. Without such an understanding, we can neither see the opportunities for change nor manage the pressures pushing for and against reform. In discussing the extremely complicated direct care "system," however, I try to strike a balance by providing enough detail on its institutions without burying the reader in unnecessary complexity. I refer the reader to the notes and appendices for more in-depth discussion and detail.

Throughout the book, I draw on a wide range of evidence, analyzing several nationally representative surveys as well as a wide range of administrative data (see appendix E for a description of my methods). In addition to these "hard" data, I conducted just under 120 interviews with a wide variety of actors in the long-term care system: direct care workers, providers, government officials at the federal and state levels, foundation staff, consultants, members of public interest groups and unions, doctors, lawyers, and insurance company representatives. The majority of the interviews were taped and transcribed, while for others I relied on careful note-taking.

Addressing the challenge of meeting the growing demand for long-term care and reforming the long-term care workforce is part of the larger topic of health care delivery, around which, it must be acknowledged, there is now considerable uncertainty owing to the outcome of the 2016 presidential election. Whatever its political fate, the (sad) fact is that the Affordable Care Act of 2010 did relatively little to address long-term care challenges, and hence there is little in this arena that can be undone by those political actors who propose repealing the act. That said, Washington will become even more passive on this front and the locus of policymaking will continue to shift to the states. If Medicaid is further devolved to the states this will become even more likely.

The argument of this book is that expanding the role of direct care workers will save the system money, both by obtaining better health outcomes—thereby reducing visits to emergency rooms, hospitals, and nursing homes—and by shifting some tasks to lower-paid occupations. This argument that costs can be reduced even as the quality of care is improved should be just as compelling to governors and legislatures as to policymakers in Washington.

A final note: although this book focuses on long-term services and supports and the direct care workers who provide them, there is an important generalization. A central challenge facing the nation is that roughly one-quarter of working adults in the United States are in poverty-level jobs.[1] What to do about the size and persistence of this large low-wage workforce is an increasingly urgent question, not just in the academic and policy worlds but also in America's politics. The stagnation of earnings and blocked mobility out of the bottom of the job market have come together to thrust an otherwise abstract discussion into the center of our national political debates.

The policy and political discussions about addressing low-wage work have focused on two main strategies: raising the minimum wage and improving the skills of the workforce. These are certainly important steps to take, but they are also inherently limited. The minimum wage will not offer a true living wage, and improving human capital will not, over any reasonable time horizon, create more good jobs.

In seeking to add to the repertoire, I have developed a strategy that I believe is a model for thinking more generally about improving low-wage work. If we are serious about transforming work and making good jobs out of bad ones, then we need to examine, on an industry-by-industry basis, the labor market circumstances of employees, the incentives facing employers, and the larger legal, political, and regulatory systems within which they operate. What combination of incentives, exposure to new ideas, availability of skilled workers, regulatory reform, and pressure will lead employers to rethink how they organize their work and structure their production? With this understanding in hand, we can think about practical strategies for upgrading the jobs of low-wage workers and improving their economic outcomes. With the aim of doing exactly this for direct care workers, this book offers a model for improving work across the board.

PART I

The State of Play

CHAPTER 1

Introduction

Many of us will need help when we get old—help with shopping, with getting dressed, with using the bathroom. Who will help us? Some people are born with developmental or physical disabilities, and others have accidents that render them unable to live a full life without assistance. Who will help those among us?

In 2015 nearly 19 million people under the age of sixty-five and nearly 14 million people over the age of sixty-five reported that they had difficulty taking care of themselves or living independently.[1] Although 33 million is a big number, it is nothing compared to what the number will be as the baby boom ages. The number of adults ages sixty-five and older who will need assistance is predicted to nearly double in the next twenty-five years (for detailed discussion of projections of future needs, see appendix D). Population growth in younger cohorts will also increase the demand for services for the non-elderly disabled.

Who will care for the aged and the younger disabled? It is beyond dispute that doctors, nurses, physical therapists, dietitians, and other professionals will be important, but we all know who does the care work on a day-to-day basis and who makes a huge difference for those who need care: unpaid family and friends, home care aides, and, in nursing homes, certified nursing assistants (CNAs).[2] Ask any adult child of an elderly parent or any parent of a younger disabled person about who is central to the quality of life and physical well-being of their loved one and they will point to these paraprofessionals.

I interviewed a social worker who told me this story about a home care aide working with an elderly woman:

> Not only did she provide the hands-on care, she did something very interesting. She looked out for the patient's welfare beyond her job . . . because toward the end of her life [the patient] had split shifts, two twelve-hour care [shifts], seven days a week, [and] if there was a new home care aide who had to come in, or someone was on vacation on the days when she was off, she would call in and talk to them about the patient's needs. The patient was difficult . . . so she would call in on her days off and make sure people understood, and [she] explained to them how you could be most successful in working with her. She put herself out tremendously.

This story tells us much about the central role of the home care aide, who earned $10 an hour, in shaping the quality of life of the patient who needed her help. But the story is also problematic in that it feeds into the belief that all that home care aides have to offer is a caring personality, warmth, and empathy. This book will argue, I hope convincingly, that home care aides can do much more and that expanding their role is the path to making the job better.

In 2007 then-senator Barack Obama spent a day "walking in their shoes" with America's employees, one of whom was a home care aide in California. The senator commented at length about how important the work was, how difficult it was, and how poorly it was compensated.[3] Seven years later, the Obama administration reinterpreted the Fair Labor Standards Act (FLSA, the federal minimum wage law) to apply to home care aides, but this change had little practical effect. Fundamentally, not much has changed since 2007.

Understanding the situation of direct care workers also speaks to another important theme: addressing the size and persistence of a large low-wage workforce in the midst of a prosperous nation. Home care aides exemplify these workers, who work on average for less than $10 an hour. Across-the-board solutions such as raising the minimum wage are certainly helpful, but to sustainably upgrade the quality of jobs, we need to understand the dynamics of each industry, the incentives of its key actors, and ways to upgrade workers' productivity so that they can earn more.

Table 1.1 The Demographics of Direct Care Workers, 2015

	CNA	Home Care Aide
Women	89.0%	88.0%
Immigrant	18.4	26.7
Under age thirty-five	44.8	28.1
Some college	49.8	46.3
Black	33.6	28.3
Hispanic	10.4	19.5

Source: 2015 American Community Survey (ACS).

CARE SETTINGS AND CARE WORKERS

Broadly speaking, caregivers fall into three groups: unpaid family members, home care aides, and CNAs. The largest group by far is made up of those unpaid family members who help their loved ones at home. I estimate that there are over 20 million such unpaid helpers (see appendix B).

Paid help at home is provided by home care aides.[4] In 2015 there were 2.2 million home care aides working "above the table." An additional unknown number worked in the so-called gray market, or "below the table." In nursing homes across the country, 1.3 million CNAs provided the vast majority of day-to-day care.

Home care aides and CNAs are similar in many respects: about 90 percent are women, and they are disproportionately people of color; while many have only a high school education, almost half have some college education. But there are also some differences between them. CNAs tend to be younger than home care aides, and about 30 percent of home care aides are immigrants; roughly 20 percent of CNAs are immigrants (see table 1.1). Median annual earnings were $15,019 in 2015 for home care aides and $20,025 for CNAs.[5] Both figures represent poverty-level earnings (for discussion of how I derived these figures, see appendix B).

Throughout the book, I take up the circumstances of all three groups of helpers—unpaid family caregivers, home care aides, and CNAs. That said, the focus does tilt toward home care aides, for two reasons. Home care aides have received relatively little attention compared to unpaid family caregivers or even CNAs. For example, an important recent Institute of Medicine (IOM) report focused on unpaid family caregivers; moreover, a large advocate community works on their behalf.[6] Similarly, and owing in part to persistent scandals and a heavier regulatory structure, there is considerably more research on CNAs than on home care aides.

A deeper explanation for my focus on home care aides—and one that points to the future—is that people prefer to stay at home and home care aides are central to making this possible. Seventy-eight percent of older people in an AARP survey strongly agreed with the statement that they wanted to stay in their home and avoid a nursing home as long as possible, and a survey by the Associated Press and the National Opinion Research Center (NORC) had exactly the same result.[7]

The younger disabled share this preference; indeed, their struggle to change society's perspective on their needs has very much the feel of a civil rights movement. A disabled woman with whom I spoke put it this way: "Younger folks want to be independent, want to live in their communities, want to do what other people do when they live their lives. They want to work, they want to go to school, whatever it is. They want to do what other people do. They're looking at as much flexibility as they can have."

A fundamental affirmation of this perspective came from the U.S. Supreme Court's ruling on the meaning of the Americans with Disabilities Act (ADA) of 1990. In the 1999 *Olmstead* decision, the Court held that institutionalization perpetuates "unwarranted assumptions" that the disabled are "incapable or unworthy of participating in community life" and "severely diminishes the everyday life activities of such individuals."[8] The Court therefore held that policy, including the provision of long-term services and support, should to the maximum degree provide the opportunity for full community and home integration.

In response to these preferences, as well as to cost considerations, public policy over the last several decades has sought to rebalance long-term services and supports (LTSS) expenditures away from nursing homes and toward home care. Enabling people to stay at home will become more difficult, however, as the pool of family caregivers shrinks relative to need (for discussion of this point, see appendix D). And while there is some debate over this point, from a public policy perspective home care is generally more cost-effective than nursing home care.[9] Of course, nursing homes will still be important when the need for care is extended and intensive, as it is for people with significant medical and self-care issues.

How Direct Care Workers Are Viewed

Direct care workers receive little respect. Decision-makers—doctors, hospitals, state regulators, state legislators, insurance companies, federal bureaucrats—typically do not think that home care aides can be real members of a care team. Home care aides are seen as unskilled companions, or glorified babysitters, with little education and little potential. Belief in them is scarce. The fact that home care aides are women and disproportionately racial minorities or immigrants does not help.

In the course of researching this book, I interviewed home care agency CEOs who made remarks like, "I totally believe the home care aides make the difference for patients, and they have not had the opportunity to show it." Such high-minded sentiments are rarely acted upon, however, and the reality on the ground is different: the work of home care aides is viewed with contempt, lack of imagination, and ignorance.

One example of contempt surfaced when I met with an expert on reforming delivery systems who worked for a nonprofit public health organization. I was interested in discussing how to fix the Medicaid program and mentioned that I was eager to expand the scope of practice for home care aides. I described the silliness of the rule in some states that home care aides cannot administer eyedrops but can only guide the hand of the client. She replied, "Well, I'm not sure the limitation is a bad idea. What if they put in the cat's eyedrops instead of the client's?" This comment came from a reasonable woman, an expert in the field, who was neither racist nor sexist. She seemed to suggest that either home care aides cannot read or they do not care enough about their clients to pay attention. (Of course no one is perfect. Consider the doctors who operate on the wrong body parts.[10] Also consider that there are no limitations on how family caregivers can administer care.)

This attitude is reflected in the policy and research communities. Consider the imbalance in research on improving nursing homes and research on improving paid home care. As mentioned earlier, the more extensive regulatory structure that governs nursing homes and the seemingly constant scandals associated with them have focused a great deal of attention on upgrading the quality of nursing homes to the point that there are now both federal and state standards and ratings. There have been systematic interventions and reform efforts, such as movements toward "culture change" and the Pioneer

Network of progressive nursing homes, which I describe later. There is simply nothing equivalent when it comes to paid home care or the role of home care aides.

In addition to contempt, there is also a great lack of imagination in understanding the role of home care aides. A doctor who runs a program aimed at expanding the role of home care aides described his vision of a home care aide as being like a "good grandmother" caring for a family. He had little sense of home care aides as real members of a care team.

Ignorance is another problematic component of the general view of home care aides. I interviewed senior administrators of the Centers for Medicare and Medicaid Services (CMS), the federal agency most responsible for funding and managing long-term care, and I also interviewed senior health care staff in the White House Office of Management and Budget (OMB). None of these senior officials had any idea about how home care is actually delivered; nor did they understand the role in long-term care of this massive workforce, which was essentially invisible to them.

Home care aides are deeply affected by these attitudes and the ignorance about their role. In a focus group, one home care aide said:

> Most people, when they hear we're a home health home care aide, they look at us like we're the scum of the earth. We're stupid. We don't know anything. I don't have to tell them nothing. I don't have to talk to them. It's bad. I'll try to tell them certain things about the client, and they act like they didn't hear anything that I said and just go straight to the client and talk to them. And I just want to say, "Hello, I'm here, I am human. . . . Home care aide is a title."

THE POSSIBLE FUTURE OF LONG-TERM CARE

Imagine that you are designing a system of care from scratch. Given people's preferences and needs, what are your goals? You know that people want to stay in their homes and remain connected to their communities, and you also know that home and community-based care is usually more affordable than institutional care. You also know that the people who spend the most time with the young and elderly disabled are home care aides. What would your system of care look like?

The most fundamental change is to reconceive long-term care as central to the quality of life of the millions of people who need it, rather than as the stepchild of the health care system, as it is seen today. This change would require raising the profile of the field within medicine and incorporating long-term care providers into health care teams. And to an important extent, the focus of medical care would have to be shifted away from a unitary interest in acute care and toward a more balanced interest in maintaining high quality of life for clients.

There are a number of concrete elements to this vision. Considering that the major source of support for people who need help is unpaid family members, you could find ways to make their lives easier and their caregiving more effective. Doing so would require thinking about broader social policies, such as paid family leave, and about more narrowly focused efforts, such as training. Most people want to stay at home, but nursing homes will continue to play an important role, and there is much room for quality improvement. Broadening access to small-group living arrangements is important. And of course, there is the challenge of financing. A great irony of our system is that the poor (via Medicaid) and the very rich have some degree of protection and insurance and the vast middle is left with nothing. As the numbers explode, this will become unacceptable.

Another part of your vision would be maximizing home care aides' contributions to the well-being of those for whom they care. As you think about ways to improve pay and working conditions for home care aides, you would look for strategies to improve their productivity and enable them to help reduce medical costs. These two objectives—ensuring that home care aides are as helpful and productive as possible and finding ways to economize on the cost of care—are complementary and point in the direction of new thinking about the delivery of care.

The central idea is to reconceive the role of home care aides. Although it is important to be realistic and not expect all aides to be interested in or capable of undertaking an expanded role, much of this book is devoted to making the case that many are in fact interested and capable. Aides could be trained in skills ranging from observation of health conditions to wound treatment to health coaching to physical therapy assistance. They could assist in clients' transitions from the hospital to the home rather than an institution. There would be regular communication between home care aides and doctors and nurses. In other words, home care aides would be members of the health care team.

This vision of the role of home care aides is far from today's reality, but it is consistent with emerging ideas about how to deliver health care. In recent years, new approaches to delivering medical care have begun to percolate through the system and gain traction. The focus has been on three key pressure points: preventative care, treatment of chronic conditions, and transitions from acute care (in hospitals) to the home. The core idea is to manage these three needs utilizing nonphysicians who work to "the top of their license." Throughout the delivery system, long-standing occupations, such as medical assistant, are being upgraded and new occupations, such as community health worker and health coach, are being implemented. In all of these cases, clinical work is done by lower-level and (importantly) cheaper employees, and the evidence shows a payoff in terms of both the quality of care and the cost. I argue here that home care aides can be part of this transformation.

One message of the emerging thinking on managing chronic conditions is that improving the quality of life for the elderly and disabled does not require high-tech medicine but rather quality care and attention. Home care aides see their clients every day for hours. No one is in a better position to help with the challenges of chronic conditions than they are.

Is integrating home care aides more deeply into the medical care team, while improving their jobs in the process, a realistic goal? Are home care aides themselves interested in these changes? Do some simply lack the capacity to learn new skills and expand their work? If substantial enhancement of their role had an impact on clients, would payers have any interest in making the investment? All of these are reasonable questions that deserve careful answers, and they will be addressed in this book.

THE DIFFICULTY OF CHANGING THE ROLE OF HOME CARE AIDES

The vision just laid out holds real promise for offering better care and improving the quality of the jobs for those who do the work. But achieving this vision will be very hard. Part of the problem—indeed a central problem—is the low repute of direct care workers, as described earlier. Lack of confidence in home care aides and respect for them is an important obstacle to expanding their role. But there are more concrete challenges. It will be no surprise to learn that a core challenge is money, on several levels. The primary funder of long-term care, not just for poor people but for some working people and middle-class people, is Medicaid.[11] Long-term care's reliance on Medicaid is a problem because Medicaid is widely seen as part of the welfare system; indeed, that is precisely where it originated. As a consequence, Medicaid funding, unlike Medicare funding, is constantly under attack and the program enjoys few powerful allies.

Medicaid is funded jointly by the federal government and the states, with the proportions varying by the wealth of the state. Thus, any effort to increase resources for the training and compensation of home care aides must go through state legislatures, which are struggling with demands on state budgets and must manage competing constituencies. This problem is not confined to "red" or "blue" states, but is a challenge that faces all states.

Compounding the problem are the incentive structures, which are not properly aligned. Most of the elderly whose long-term care is paid by Medicaid are also covered by Medicare, but the Medicaid system, being partly funded by states and subject to state policymaking, has no incentive to save Medicare costs (by, for example, enhancing the role of aides), since Medicare is entirely federally funded. It is essential that these incentives be fixed, and some efforts are being made to do so.

The third obstacle lies in politics, especially occupational politics. Scholars who study occupations have long noted the sharp elbows and jostling for position when two occupations seek to capture the same set of tasks. Lawyers and real estate agents, for instance, have fought over their spheres of control, as have plumbers and pipefitters. Any effort to expand the role of home care aides is quickly reminded that nurses are no friend of such an expansion. In most states the nurse practice act (NPA) sharply limits what home care aides can do, as illustrated later when I describe recent efforts to create an "advanced aide" title in New York State. This example even understates the problem, considering how modest the proposed upgrades were that would have qualified a home care aide as an advanced aide. There has been no serious effort to enact the vision laid out here, and certainly such an effort would raise substantial opposition.

The lack of alignment between the interests of the two main stakeholders, the elderly and the younger disabled, only compounds these political difficulties. The disability movement is best understood as a drive for civil rights, one strong theme of which has been an insistence by the disabled on controlling and managing their own care to the maximum extent possible and avoiding any whiff of "medicalization" or "doctor knows best." A slogan of the movement, "nothing about us without us" captures this theme. The aversion of the disability rights movement to medicalization and expert control is understandable, but the movement's implied opposition to policies aimed at expanding the role of home care aides and deepening their responsibilities and training works against the interests of the other stakeholder, the elderly. This potential fracture in a coalition of the elderly, the disabled, and home care aides weakens any movement to address the failings of the current system.

REASONS TO BE OPTIMISTIC

Although there are many challenges to improving long-term care and the role of home care aides, there are also reasons to think that progress is possible.

Simple demographics will push us toward a solution. As the number of people who need care rises and the reservoir of family caregivers shrinks, rising pressures toward reforming the system are likely to be translated into politics. The structure of the long-term care industry is also changing. All states are moving their Medicaid long-term care into managed care insurance (and out of the traditional fee-for-service systems), and calls for integrating Medicaid and Medicare systems for the elderly are increasing. State budgets are under pressure, and states' share of Medicaid long-term care costs is a big part of the problem. We can therefore hope that both insurance companies and the states will consider the feasibility of using the relatively cheap services of home care aides, once they are better trained and have a broader set of duties, to reduce the costs of chronic care in lieu of more expensive health care providers. In states where they are active, unions are pushing to expand the role of home care aides. Add all of this up and the potential is there to shake up a stagnant system, improve the options of those who need assistance, and make far better use of the human capital and potential of home care aides.

THE BROADER CONTEXT: ADDRESSING INCOME INEQUALITY AND THE COST OF CARE

Our country's ability to provide long-term care is faced with many challenges: it is expensive and beyond the means of most Americans; the delivery system is fragmented and very difficult to navigate; and families are under enormous stress and must often make considerable sacrifices to care for their loved ones. Fixing this system will bring us closer, however, to addressing two of the most important challenges our society faces: maintaining and indeed improving the quality of life for our soon-to-explode elderly and disabled populations, and addressing growing economic cleavages and the persistence of a large low-wage job economy.

Activists, researchers, and policymakers have noted and deplored the circumstances of direct care workers, both those in homes and those in nursing homes. What I add is a framework for thinking about the problem and some analysis and data to flesh it out; most importantly, I place this challenge in the context of our larger system of long-term care. I describe how the job market for aides functions; lay out the financing and industrial system that shapes the present system and constrains improvement; offer evidence that transforming the role of aides can improve the overall quality of long-term care and save money; address the economic and political challenges of making this happen, and offer a vision of a long-term care system that is both more humane and more effective. I argue that improvement is possible if we align our interest in improving the jobs of direct care workers with the goal of improving care for clients and helping payers and providers operate more efficiently and profitably. Moreover, this in-depth analysis of the industry and its economic and political context provides a model for thinking about how to improve the quality of low-wage jobs in other settings.

As a nation, we spend too much on health care, and those costs are not sustainable. One approach is to cut care and ration it, but most of us would agree that this is not the way to go. We need to find ways to deliver quality care for less money. One component of the solution is to increase productivity by reallocating tasks. As a recent *New England Journal of Medicine* article on the health care system argued:

Approaches that encourage delegation of tasks from physicians and nurses to other workers . . . provide opportunities for additional savings and increased productivity. . . . A large obstacle to such a wholesale redesign is the complexity of the federal and state reimbursement rules and requirements for scope of practice, licensure, and staffing ratios.[12]

This is precisely the argument developed in this book. By expanding the role of aides, not only do we improve their jobs and reduce the incidence of low-wage work in America, but we can also improve the delivery of care and save money while doing it.

This is not to say that the choices will be easy. Much of this reform effort will be conducted in the weeds of policy; appeals to fairness and decency, no matter how evocative, have to be matched by a deep understanding of the mechanics of the system and the incentives motivating all of the actors. At the same time, if we can demonstrate the path toward better practice in such a way as to motivate a powerful coalition of consumers and workers, then we will all be better off.

THE PLAN OF THE BOOK

To say that the challenges facing our provision of long-term care are complicated would be a radical understatement, and part I describes the present landscape in the depth we need in order to begin meeting those challenges. The next chapter provides an overview of that landscape, including the key institutions and the vocabulary of long-term and direct care. In chapter 3, I describe the world of direct care workers: who they are and the work they do. Chapter 4 takes up the labor market for aides, and chapter 5 discusses unpaid family caregivers and the important topic of the consumer-directed model, under which families receive support to hire their own home care aides, who are also typically family members.

In part II, I turn to the future. Chapter 6 briefly introduces the question of whether it is in fact reasonable to think that the role of aides can be expanded. Chapter 7 reviews the arguments for taking this path as well as the evidence that it can work. I believe that the material in this chapter is convincing and that a fair-minded reading supports the idea that a new approach to the provision of long-term care is possible. But reason does not always win out: chapter 8 describes the obstacles, economic and political and cultural, to change. There are also reasons to be optimistic, however, and these are the topic of chapter 9. I conclude the book with a discussion of concrete steps for moving ahead.

CHAPTER 2

The Landscape of Long-Term Care in the United States

The American system of long-term care is enormously complicated. People receive care under diverse arrangements, caregivers work under varied circumstances, financing is a patchwork of different systems, and the industry is highly decentralized and varied. Adding to the complexity is that, for services financed by Medicaid, each of the fifty states has discretion regarding eligibility standards, reimbursement rates, and the mix of services offered.

This brief chapter provides a kind of pocket roadmap of the patchwork long-term care system, identifying the actors and describing the programs that, taken together, form the system. Much of what is sketched here will be elaborated in greater depth as we proceed. But moving forward through this analysis of the system will be facilitated with this quick guide in hand. In addition, some of the important numbers are provided in the accompanying list.

Number of Direct Care Workers, 2015

Paid home care aides: 2,199,893

Certified nursing assistants: 1,288,000

Unpaid family caregivers: 20,659,915[1]

Median Annual Earnings, 2015

Home care aides: $15,019

Certified nursing assistants: $20,025[2]

Number of Disabled, 2015

Under age sixty-five: 18,810,861

Age sixty-five and older: 13,923,663[3]

Costs

Total spending for LTSS, 2013: $310 billion

Spent by Medicaid: 51 percent

Spent by other public sources of funding: 21 percent

Paid out of pocket: 19 percent

Paid by private insurance: 8 percent[4]

WHO NEEDS LONG-TERM CARE?

There are multiple criteria for determining who needs long-term care. With respect to functional limitations, the conventional categories are so-called activities of daily living (ADLs) and instrumental activities of daily living (IADLs). The former include eating, dressing, bathing, mobility, and toileting, while the latter are activities such as shopping, cooking, and doing errands.

The definitional issues center on just how many and what type of disabilities add up to the need for care. There are also broader descriptions of disability, such as difficulty with mobility or difficulty with self-care. In addition, a person's age makes a difference: how one measures disabilities differs for a three-year-old and a sixty-five-year-old. Finally, even if these definitions were universally agreed upon, different surveys yield different answers.

Appendix A walks through these definitions in depth and provides alternative estimates of who needs long-term care. That said, my preferred estimate for 2015 is that 142,000 people ages zero to four were disabled, 945,000 people ages five to fourteen were disabled, and 31,647,000 people ages fifteen and older were disabled. Of the total disabled population, fewer than half, 13,923,000, were ages sixty-five and older.

WHO PROVIDES LONG-TERM CARE?

Unpaid family care is by far the most common source of care. Although there are varying estimates of the number of family members providing care (whom

I discuss in more detail in chapter 3 and appendix B), my own estimate is that in 2012 there were 20.6 million unpaid family and friend caregivers.

Paid care at home is provided by the group I term "home care aides." The 2015 American Community Survey (ACS) counted 2.1 million aides, of whom nearly 90 percent were women and close to one-third were immigrants. These figures underestimate the number of paid aides, for two reasons. First, those people whose main job is working as a home care aide but who work under the table are unlikely to report to a census-taker that they are working. This is the so-called gray market, the size of which is unknown. Second, the count of "above-the-table" home care aides is based on census occupational reports in which people identify their main job, but this does not capture those people who report the occupational title of a different main job, who moonlight as a home care aide, and who report their income from being a home care aide to the Internal Revenue Service (IRS) (and hence are not in the gray market).

The general term "home care aide" obscures a distinction between two subgroups. One subgroup is home health aides, who are required by federal regulation to receive seventy-five hours of training and are eligible to be reimbursed by Medicare for helping clients in post-acute care situations (for example, for short periods of time after leaving a hospital). There is no federal training requirement for the second subgroup, personal care assistants (the exact term varies by state), and it is up to each state to decide whether they must receive any training.

Home health aides can perform minor medical tasks (such as changing dressings and taking vital signs) if they are trained and supervised by a nurse, but the allowable tasks vary considerably from state to state, depending on the state's nurse practice act. The AARP, which keeps track of what is permitted in each state, reports that, for example, thirty-one permit home health aides to administer oral medicine but nineteen do not.[5] In all states, however, permission to perform any medical task is client-specific and does not extend to other clients.

Although these distinctions can occasionally be important, they rarely are. As a practical matter, most home health aides and personal care assistants end up doing the same work: helping with ADLs and IADLs and providing companionship but not help with medical tasks. Throughout the book, I refer to both groups as home care aides.

ORGANIZATIONAL ARRANGEMENTS FOR
PROVIDING CARE

Paid help is provided by agencies, by paid family members, and via informal networks that operate both above and below the table with respect to tax authorities.

Many agencies that provide paid help are small local organizations, but national chains are increasingly operating in the field (and a few operate on-line as virtual agencies).[6] In 2012 there were over 56,000 establishments in the two main industry classifications that capture home care, and this figure represented a very substantial increase since the last Economic Census of the United States in 2007, a period when, by contrast, the overall number of establishments in the American economy declined.[7] The Economic Census also shows that the sector has become dominated by for-profit establishments: in 2012, there were over 41,000, compared to about 14,000 not subject to federal taxes. All the growth between 2007 and 2012 was accounted for by the for-profit establishments.[8]

Agencies vary considerably in their funding source, the clients they seek out, and their size and geographical scope. At one end of the spectrum are small local agencies that depend on Medicaid (and sometimes Medicare), and at the other end are national chains that cater to clients who either can pay out of pocket or have long-term care insurance and that offer a spectrum of care services, including home care aides but also nurses, social workers, and care coordinators. The industry is not concentrated: in the category "elderly and disabled services," the top four providers accounted for less than 5 percent of revenue in 2015.[9] Another piece of evidence along these lines is that 40 percent of agencies that rely on private pay or long-term insurance have just one location.[10]

The second source of paid home care is family members. In addition to whatever informal compensation arrangements family members might work out among themselves (and there are no data on this), about 850,000 family members are paid with Medicaid funds via consumer-directed programs.[11] This funding system permits clients to forgo an agency and choose whom they want to hire; as a matter of practice, family and friends are the primary choice. (See chapter 5 for a discussion of consumer-directed programs.)

Networks of home care aides are the final source of paid help. Many aides are self-employed and report themselves as such to both the Census and tax authorities, but some of them operate under the table, and therefore it is difficult to know their prevalence. In the next chapter and in appendix B, I estimate the size of this "hidden" workforce.

NURSING HOMES AND ASSISTED LIVING

In 2014, there were 15,400 nursing homes in the United States, a slight decline from 16,100 in 2004. Just under 69 percent of nursing homes in 2014 were for-profit, and over half were owned by chains. A relatively small number (1.3 million) and percentage (3.6 percent) of the population ages sixty-five and older in 2014 lived in an institutional setting such as a nursing home.[12] About three times this number will pass through a nursing home over the course of a year. However, that proportion increases dramatically with age, ranging from 1 percent for people ages sixty-five to seventy-four years to 3 percent for people ages seventy-five to eighty-four and 11 percent for people ages eighty-five and older.[13]

The number of residents in nursing homes has been steadily declining, but research literature on just why this is happening is limited.[14] The decline in usage is probably due in part not only to individual preferences but also to the "rebalancing" of public policies, which have shifted resources into home care and made support for home care easier to access. An additional consideration is the emergence of assisted living as a more palatable alternative to nursing homes.[15]

Medicaid was the primary payer in 2014 for 62 percent of nursing home residents; 14 percent were covered by Medicare (which reimburses at a much higher rate for short-term rehabilitation stays and hence accounts for a larger fraction of total revenue) and 23 percent paid either with private insurance or out of pocket.[16]

Nursing home inspections revealed that, in 2014, 20 percent of facilities were deficient in ways that put residents' health in jeopardy.[17] Recent research utilizing random assignment to control for patient health status and demographics suggests that patients treated in hospitals with high rates of discharge into nursing homes have poorer survival rates than patients in hospitals that avoid nursing homes.[18] Nursing home scandals are a regular feature in the press.

These worries notwithstanding, nursing homes will continue to be an important component of long-term services and supports. The good news is that in recent years standards have been tightened and a number of promising national models (described in chapter 7) have emerged that offer better quality care. And of course, nursing homes employ large numbers of certified nursing assistants whose wages and working conditions are only marginally better than those of home care aides.

Assisted living (often called "residential care" in the literature) is a more complicated sector because it encompasses a range of formats, but the official definition is a facility that offers four or more beds, two or more meals a day, and round-the-clock supervision. In 2010, there were 31,000 assisted living facilities, with 970,000 beds (compared to many fewer nursing homes but considerably more nursing home beds).[19]

Assisted living residents need help along a variety of dimensions, but there are no specific health-related entrance requirements for assisted living facilities. By contrast, nursing homes funded by Medicaid or insurance typically require that residents suffer from at least two ADL challenges or cognitive disability. In 2010, only 11 percent of assisted living facilities were willing to admit people with skilled nursing needs; in fact, according to the SCAN Foundation, assisted living facilities have become less willing over time to admit people with ADL needs and more likely to discharge people who develop such needs.[20] That said, recent data indicate that assisted living residents need more care and suffer from more health problems than the typical elderly person living in their community, but are in considerably better shape than the typical nursing home resident.[21] For example, in 2011, 74 percent of people ages sixty-five and older living in an assisted living facility received help with self-care or mobility.[22] Unlike nursing homes, where about two-thirds of residents are covered by Medicaid, only 19 percent of assisted living residents receive Medicaid support.[23]

Assisted living has emerged as an important alternative to traditional nursing homes. Although typically assisted living facilities are not permitted to offer skilled nursing care, many get around this limitation by contracting out to visiting nurse associations. Assisted living cannot replace nursing homes for the frailest people and those in need of intensive care, but it can drain off the demand for services from those in less acute condition, particularly people who can pay from their own resources.

LOOKING AHEAD: THE DEMAND FOR LONG-TERM CARE AND THE SUPPLY OF AIDES

The aging of the baby boom generation will radically increase the demand for long-term care while at the same time the number of people available to provide that care will shrink. These core demographic facts will shape much of the policymaking and politics with respect to long-term care. In chapter 9 and appendix D, I analyze these trends in more detail, but here it is sufficient to note that, by my calculations, in 2030 we will face a shortfall of over hundreds of thousands of direct care workers and several million unpaid family caregivers. By 2040, these shortfalls will grow to nearly 350,000 and 11 million, respectively. Furthermore, for reasons laid out in the appendix, I regard these estimates as overly conservative.

WHO PAYS FOR LONG-TERM CARE?

Experts disagree about the exact total cost of long-term care, but one estimate puts that figure at $310 billion in 2013.[24] Nearly 20 percent of this cost was paid by people out of their own pockets. Insurance covered 8 percent of the total, and the remaining 72 percent was financed via publicly funded programs, of which over two-thirds was Medicaid.

The conventional wisdom among analysts of long-term care is that Medicare is not part of the story, based on the explicit Medicare rule that the program pays only for short episodes of home care or nursing home care after acute incidents, such as discharge from a hospital or upon doctor's orders. This is correct, but it misses an important point. If we think about Medicare from the viewpoint of clients and their families, then to a certain extent this distinction is not relevant. True, Medicare cannot pay for extended care, but long-term care is often not truly extended. Users of long-term care utilize support for an average of three years (see appendix A), and given that doctors can renew their orders and individuals may have multiple hospital visits, and hence multiple discharges, Medicare should be considered a component of the system. Medicaid still dominates, and Medicare cannot support extended, continuous long-term care, but it is relevant.

The other non-Medicaid sources of funding for long-term care are private insurance and out-of-pocket payment. The market for long-term insurance is small: just under 12 percent of people between the ages of forty and seventy have some form of long-term care insurance, and this level of market penetration has not changed in the past decade. Furthermore, policies are expensive (the average annual premium is over $2,000), have limited benefits, and require a waiting period of 90 to 100 days before benefits kick in.[25] As a result, private insurance accounts for only 8 percent of total spending on long-term care.[26]

It is obviously difficult to accurately measure the extent to which people pay out of pocket for long-term care, but common sense and observation of our own family and friends would suggest that the figure is substantial. This impression is substantiated by data in the Health and Retirement Survey (HRS) (which captures the situation only of people ages fifty and older): 33.8 percent of respondents who received paid help paid that cost (or their family paid it) out of pocket. Even among those who reported that some form of insurance or public support covered some of the costs, 22 percent still contributed out of pocket. The median out-of-pocket expenditure was over $450 a month, and one-quarter of the respondents paid $800 a month out of pocket.[27] Clearly out-of-pocket expenditures are an important part of the story.

WHO RECEIVES MEDICAID SUPPORT FOR LONG-TERM SERVICES AND SUPPORTS?

Given that Medicaid is a welfare program, it should be no surprise that eligibility is driven by income and assets, with the emphasis being on having little of each. What is difficult to navigate—and supports a large legal establishment—are the enormous complications surrounding this simple idea. Happily for our focus on the provision of services and the nature of the industry, it suffices to work with a general understanding of eligibility.[28]

In every state, eligibility for Medicaid support for long-term care is determined by income, assets, and the extent of the applicant's functional disability. States must provide support to people whose income is no higher than the standard for receiving Supplemental Security Income (SSI), and states can opt to extend this income limit up to 300 percent of SSI—in 2016, $2,999 a month for an individual. The typical asset limits are $2,000 for an individual and $3,000 for a couple. Individuals may "spend down" their income and assets on medical or long-term care to meet these standards. States determine the functional standards, but typically they involve the degree of self-care assistance needed.

Under federal rules, states must provide nursing home support to people who meet these criteria, but increasingly states are seeking to encourage the use of home care because it can be less expensive. Whereas in the past a person had to meet nursing home standards of functional need to obtain support for home and community-based services (HCBS), federal waivers of legislated rules, as well as provisions in the Affordable Care Act (ACA), offer more flexibility for HCBS eligibility but also permit waitlists and tighter definitions of eligible subgroups.

It is important to note that, in reality, the asset standards for home care are more generous than the $2,000/$3,000 limit, and that for married couples the spouse who does not need care can have additional assets (for example, their home) as well as higher income.

In 2014, Medicaid support was received by 1.4 million people for nursing home residence and by 3.2 million for home care.[29] In 2014, across thirty-nine states, 582,000 people were on waitlists for home and community-based services.[30] In terms of budget distribution, home care accounted for a bit over 51 percent of Medicaid spending.[31] The data are clear that access to Medicaid does increase the chances that people will receive long-term services and supports.[32]

A final point regarding eligibility concerns the politically fraught question of whether people with assets above the limits are able to maneuver their way into the Medicaid support system. It is clear that people commonly "spend down" and that those whose income and assets are initially above the limits do receive support. Whether people well above the limits are able to utilize the system is less clear. There are multiple strands of research that take up this question, but the answer remains inconclusive.[33]

OTHER IMPORTANT ACTORS IN LONG-TERM CARE

Several other actors play important roles in the world of long-term care. Since Medicaid is a federal-state program, policymakers at both levels of government shape the rules and regulations and determine funding levels. In the several states where home care aides are unionized, the unions are significant actors. Advocates also play a role—for example, the AARP speaking for the elderly and various disability organizations speaking for their constituencies. In addition, what might be termed public interest organizations are important, most notably PHI (formerly the Paraprofessional Healthcare Institute) and the National Domestic Workers Alliance (NDWA).

THE LEGAL STRUCTURE THAT GOVERNS THE LONG-TERM SYSTEM

The overall system of support for long-term care is a hodgepodge of arrangements, with no single overarching regulatory structure. That said, it is subject to some important laws and regulations. The Fair Labor Standards Act sets standards with respect to the minimum wage and overtime. Some states have established training requirements for home care aides who are not covered by Medicare regulations. The Americans with Disabilities Act has been interpreted by the Supreme Court to require the maximum feasible efforts to enable disabled people to live in communities rather than in institutions. And of course, the federal government has enacted a range of regulations regarding Medicaid and Medicare.

A NOTE ON DATA

Throughout this book, I draw on a number of surveys and other data sources, but two that I use extensively are the 2015 American Community Survey and the 2012 Health and Retirement Survey. The ACS is a nationally representative census survey of all Americans, including those in institutions.[34] The HRS is a nationally representative survey of people ages fifty and older who live at home.[35] For more detail regarding data and research methods, see appendix E.

CHAPTER 3

The Direct Care Workforce

The husband of a client: It got to the point when life became unmanageable for all of us. . . . The caregivers care . . . with incredible generosity of spirit and patience and love.

A home care aide: I get up about five in the morning, then I take the bus to the train, and then I work the eight hours here, seven to three-thirty. Then I need to go to my second job. I take two buses to get there. I need to be there from four to midnight. My second job is because my son started in college.

A trainer: Paid caregivers are forgotten, so forgotten. We have lots of programs for family members, we all know this disease takes its toll on family members. You hear that all the time. But you never hear anyone say this disease takes its toll on home health home care aides. Sometimes the home care aides don't even know, they just say, "I'm tired all the time." . . . And they also have their own lives.

From interviews at the New York Alzheimer's Association

It is important not to be naive. Certainly there are home care aides who only go through the motions, or even worse, who abuse or take advantage of clients. Well-designed systems can prevent this to some degree, but nothing can protect against someone who may meet minimal competency expectations but is indifferent or mean. That said, the home care aides I met were committed to their clients, emotionally involved, and, in training sessions, eager to learn how to improve care. I interviewed aides, attended training sessions with dozens of them, and watched tapes of other training sessions. They all found their work rewarding and satisfying, if also physically and emotionally grueling. But they also felt disrespected and undervalued and knew that they could contribute to the care team well beyond what was permitted.

In this chapter, I describe who these aides are, what they do, how they are viewed, and their working conditions. I draw on both national surveys and my interviews with direct care workers, providers, insurance companies, government officials, and advocates. I discuss unpaid family caregivers, as well as those who are hired and compensated under consumer-directed programs, in chapter 5.

HOME CARE AIDES

Let's start with the example of a home care aide in New York. You have received between forty and seventy-five hours of training, depending on your exact title (in many other states the range is zero to seventy-five hours), and you are now assigned to care for a disabled person in his or her home. You have been given a care plan, and a nurse has probably visited the client to help design it. But it is likely to be another six months before a nurse or other support person visits you and your client. Your client may be a young disabled person who is fully cognizant of his or her needs and can direct you in how to help. Or your client may be a physically capable older person with dementia who is stubborn and abusive. Or perhaps your client is someone with multiple sclerosis who has good days and very bad days. You may have to lift and carry your client. (Modern nursing homes have machinery for this, but you are on your own in the home.) Your client may have a family who helps, or no family, or a family who thinks you are the maid and gives you their laundry to clean. Your client may have daily medical needs—pills to take or wounds to care for—or destructive health habits that, if addressed, would make a big difference. If the client begins to exhibit troubling symptoms, or even something as manageable as a bed sore, you are not allowed to do anything "medical" (unless you are providing care through a consumer-directed program). You can call the office in the hope of speaking to a care coordinator, although it is far more likely that you will get an answering machine. Or you can call 911 and go to the emergency room, an option that is easy but very expensive.

The bottom line is clear: you were quickly trained and now you are alone. You make around $11 an hour, and you may have two assignments this day, or perhaps you are working a twelve-hour shift. Your schedule could be different in a few months.

Home care aides help clients with what are termed activities of daily living (ADLs), such as dressing, toileting, and bathing, as well as with so-called instrumental activities of daily living (IADLs), such as cooking and shopping. They also provide companionship. Gertrude, who had come to the United States from Jamaica twenty years ago and had been working as a home care aide ever since, described this aspect of her job. She had been with her current client for eight years, and she worked eight hours every weekday and every other weekend. She said:

> I love my job! I love taking care of people, and I love what I do. I put everything into it . . . there are challenges, but I'm up to my challenge. My client has MS, and sometimes it's very difficult for her. But I try to make her as comfortable as possible. As I said before, they have their bad days and they have their good days. I try to be there for her, whether it's a bad or good day. Second thing is that she has a son, which I help out sometimes at the store or do little things for him. I am not there for the son, but because it's *her* son, I try to help with a little bit. It's the person I am.

Although home care aides are responsible for calling for help, they are typically not allowed to do anything proactive with respect to the health of the client. The core point, and one I will return to repeatedly, is that they are not seen as part of the medical care team. These restrictions flow from nurse delegation laws in each state and the related scope of practice restrictions. Indeed, these tensions go as far back as the New Deal, when home care aides were employed by the Works Progress Administration (WPA) as a form of poor relief. The historians Eileen Boris and Jennifer Klein report that "State Nurses Association and the Board of Nurse Examiners drew the line where 'simple home care' ended and nursing began. . . . Excluded [for home care aides] were 'installation of nasal or eye drops, applications of dressings, bandages, or poultices . . . electric lamps, heating pads, simple types of massage, preparation of infant formulas, helping the patient apply a brace. . . .' "[1]

Because limitations on what home care aides can do are formalized and not simply a matter of common practice, they cannot be easily modified. Thinking this through and shifting the boundaries is, as I explained in the first chapter, the key to improving the jobs of home care aides and improving the care of the people they help, but for now I limit myself to descriptions of current reality. And here is how crazy it can get, as described by an agency supervisor of home care aides whom I interviewed. I asked him about eyedrops:

> To be specific, Paul, assisting is not [the aides] actually putting in the eyedrops. They would place the eyedrop in the client's hand and put their hand over the client's hand, and [they] can guide them to put the drops in the eye. That's the difference between assisting versus if they were actually administering the eyedrops.

Exceptions to scope of practice restrictions do exist. There are no limitations on the medical activities of home care aides who work under consumer-directed programs, in which the client hires and supervises and often trains the home care aide (other than, of course, what they are capable of doing). The same is true for private-pay home care aides: if you hire a home care aide and pay her out of your own pocket, she can do whatever you wish her to. However, if you hire a private-pay home care aide via an agency, it is likely that the agency will enforce the scope of practice limitations.

Lack of Respect

Closely connected to the inability of home care aides to perform even the simplest medical tasks is the lack of respect for them from both medical professionals and insurance companies. They are not taken seriously as members of the care team. As a result, it is very difficult to make a case for expanding their jobs and compensating them commensurately. This disrespect has several roots, including racism, sexism, medical elitism, and turf protection on the part of other health care occupations. Overcoming these attitudes and convincing an insurance company or a hospital system that home care aides can do more will require compelling evidence, and I offer such evidence in a later chapter. But here it is important to note that in their daily work home care aides are acutely aware of the disrespect aimed at them, they are hurt by it, and they resent it.

This lack of respect also has deep historical roots. Eileen Boris and Jennifer Klein describe the origins of the current system in the WPA's Visiting House-keeping Program during the New Deal and subsequently in the emerging welfare system put in place in the 1960s as part of the War on Poverty. The employment of home care aides was viewed as a form of workfare: providing jobs to poor women who would otherwise simply collect welfare.[2] Home care aides were poor women who needed work, and the work they were given was taking care of the elderly poor. The long-standing (and only very recently remedied) exclusion of home care aides from coverage under the FLSA (minimum wage and overtime protection) reflects this perspective. Doubly stigmatized—the poor tending the poor—home care has never fully escaped this image.

Home care aides, as one very knowledgeable observer said to me, are the "stepchild of health care." Another observer, a nurse leading a major teaching hospital's efforts to improve long-term care by developing specialty nurses, said that "no one pays attention to home care aides or CNAs. When something changes, they notice but are not taken seriously. They can see changes in condition. They can sense family discord. [They] should be eyes and ears but are not. Sad, because they are [a] big source of patient satisfaction, and this is increasingly important for providers."

Even high-level policy officials demonstrated a dismissive view of home care aides. One person I spoke with said that the key to understanding home care aides is to realize that many of them want "fictive kin" and hence are less focused on improving their economic situation than advocates presume. I interviewed very senior CMS and OMB officials who essentially knew nothing about the status of home care aides, their training, or the possibilities regarding their potential role on the health team.

This lack of knowledge or insight about home care aides is reflected in the research and demonstration world. Billions of dollars are spent annually on testing innovations in health care delivery, yet there is virtually no large-scale, federally supported research looking at strategies for enhancing the role of home care aides. There are a few federally funded training demonstrations, but they make no effort to alter the scope of practice, they permit each site to design its own intervention, and they typically do not measure client outcomes. A recent review of the literature on home health outcomes also revealed this blind spot with respect to home care aides: the literature is all about nurses and social workers, with virtually no discussion of home care aides.[3]

Home care aides are aware of these attitudes. As one aide put it, "Our title holds us back a lot." They felt a similar lack of respect from other health professionals with whom they interacted. When I asked a group of home care aides about their relationship with supervisors, nurses, and physical therapists, they commented:

> Supervisor needs to listen to you when you call and not put you on hold for a very long time. You can only do one thing at a time, and they *need to be a little more polite.*

> Get people who love to do their job and *not speak to people like if they were nobody.* They need to learn that without us they won't have a job.

> They can improve the way they take care of problems. *No one hears you out.*

In a focus group I conducted among home care aides who were in a health coach training class, I asked if they felt that they could do more than they were allowed to do. They all shouted "Yes!" and said that they felt disrespected. "Unless someone is hurt, no one pays attention to us," one aide said. "We know everything about the patient, but nurse and supervisor don't listen," added another. And yet another noted, "We are the eyes and the ears." They told stories about reporting issues with clients and receiving no response. "You make reports and they don't make a move."

A dramatic story about being ignored was told to me by a home care aide who was so committed to her client that on her own unpaid time she visited her in the hospital. She knew that the client was experiencing pain in one arm, and she also knew that the client was too ill to explain the issue to the hospital staff, so she tried to explain about the client's arm pain. "When I told them, they said, 'You are the relative?' And I said, 'No, but I am her home health home care aide.' And they threw me out. They said, 'You are not the relative. Go out. We have to work with her. Get out.'"

Desire to Learn

Home care aides may not be respected, but the fact is that they want to do more. The aides I interviewed almost uniformly said that they loved their jobs. When I asked in a focus group what they liked about their work, their responses were all in the same vein: they enjoyed "helping people," "the smile on their faces," "knowing I'm doing something for someone else." In every training session I attended, home care aides were attentive and clearly wanting to learn.

These were training sessions that home care aides had volunteered to attend in order to deepen their skills. During one break, I asked why they were participating. "To do a better job," they said, and "to learn for the patient." Also, "I like to learn more." They viewed the scope of practice limitations as ridiculous: of course they were capable of putting in eyedrops, helping with physical therapy exercises, or tending wounds. "It's always good to know more, just helping her do her everyday chores. . . . I would like to be able to help her to be more independent. I could be trained to change the dressing. I could do what the visiting nurse does. I could learn those skills."

Compensation

The median income for home care aides in 2015 was $15,019, which is shockingly low.[4] It is very hard to make a good living in this job: only one-quarter of home care aides made more than $20,430 in 2015, and only 10 percent of all home care aides made more than $30,043. If we look only at those home care aides who managed to find full-year, full-time work (one-third of the total), median earnings were still a paltry $22,428. This figure is below the poverty line for a family of four. Moreover, the payoff to home care aides for obtaining any formal education beyond high school is only an additional 9 percent a year, compared to a boost of 45 percent for the workforce as a whole.[5]

Working Conditions

Isolation is inherent in the home care aide's job: after all, the aide is alone in the home with the client. But the nature of the systems around the home care aide intensifies the isolation. Typically, because a nurse visits the home only once every six months or so, the home care aide is dependent on the agency's care coordinator. But this person has a very large caseload and is often hard to reach. Home care aides told many stories of their calls not being returned, or calls being returned hours later and in the interim the aide had been left alone to deal with a difficult problem. The result was either the client continuing to be at risk or an unnecessary 911 call and an expensive visit to the ER. Some home care aides identified this problem as a communication issue:

> Our work would be easier if the coordinators would furnish us with precise information about the clients; give to us not only the direction to get to the clients, but his/her health condition. . . . The supervisors in general send us to a dark and blank situation where we have to figure out what to do. If we call them [the supervisor] back to report the situation, normally we have an attitude as help.

> Communication!!! It's hard for me to get in touch with my supervisor, and I am unaware of a lot of things and my patients are the ones telling me.

Besides isolation, the working conditions of home care aides put them at risk in two other ways as well. Some of their work is physical—lifting clients, for example—and this kind of work day in and day out clearly makes them susceptible to injuries. And working in isolation, they have little protection from clients who are abusive or even violent.

The evidence regarding injuries is compelling. The Bureau of Labor Statistics (BLS) reports that home care aides lost workdays owing to injuries at nearly twice the rate of all private industry workers.[6] A recent analysis of workers' compensation claims in Washington State found that home health workers were injured 50 percent more frequently than workers in all other industries.[7] The issue is sufficiently serious that the Centers for Disease Control and Prevention (CDC) recently issued a report providing guidance on how to reduce the injury rate of home health workers.[8]

A recent survey of home care aides in Oregon's consumer-directed program found high levels of physical violence (14 percent reported someone trying to hit them) or sexual harassment (21 percent were inappropriately exposed to sexual materials), and national surveys find a similar pattern.[9]

The Search for Hours

Talking with home care aides makes it clear that for many of them the number-one issue is hours. This concern may seem paradoxical given the growing demand for services. But it comes from the nature of that demand and the organization of the industry. Insurance companies assess clients to determine how many hours of assistance they need; although a universal assessment tool is widely used, in reality the relationship between the assessment of need and the assignment of hours to meet that need is in the hands of the payer, which of course has an incentive to limit help. And truth be told, many people who need help do not need it all day long. As a consequence, most cases do not provide full-time work, and home care aides have to piece together multiple cases, which can be difficult.[10]

The most important thing [the agency] could do to make my job better is to find me a *permanent case right now which requires seven or eight hours per day*. Right now, I am on a permanent case for four hours per day, and that is not enough. I can hardly [get] by with twenty hours per week. I called on every occasion, telling them I need more hours, and to no avail, they keep saying nothing is available at the moment, yet they keep recruiting [home health aides] every two months. I need seven or eight hours per day!

Give me *longer cases than three-hour cases*. I work every day and don't even make part-time. Twenty-one hours is not enough, but thirty hours is okay. Four hours here, three hours there, I don't like this at all, but I'm accepting it for now.

In the American Community Survey, only half of home care aides reported that they worked full-time—that is, thirty-five or more hours a week. The Health and Retirement Survey asks each respondent (or the respondent's surrogate) about the number of hours worked by his or her helper, and figure 3.1

Figure 3.1   Distribution of Hours for Paid Home Care Aides, 2012

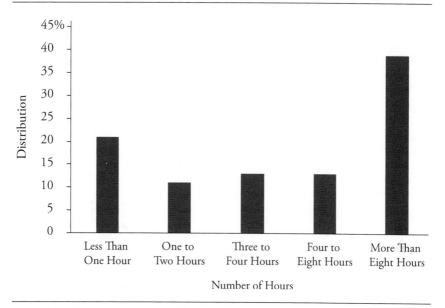

Source: 2012 Health and Retirement Survey (HRS).
Note: Data refer to home care aides' clients age fifty or older.

shows the data for paid home care aides in 2012. Most helpers worked well under full-time hours for any given client, and it is clear that piecing together a full-time job is a significant challenge for home care aides.

CERTIFIED NURSING ASSISTANTS

Certified nursing assistants, the equivalent of home care aides in nursing homes, are demographically very similar to home care aides. The earnings of CNAs are slightly better than those of home care aides, largely because nursing homes historically have been better funded (this is changing) and are more likely to be unionized.

In her ethnographic account of a nursing home, Nancy Foner describes an environment with strong bureaucratic rules, close supervision, intense time pressures, and clients who tend to be considerably more difficult to work with than the typical home-based client:

One diligent and conscientious worker complained "you cut corners because you can't do everything they assign you in one day." Another aide had an hour and a quarter after lunch before quitting time in which she had to give one bath, put two patients back to bed, change two, and do her paperwork. "I never have enough time to sit and talk with patients, always rushing. I guess that's how they want it."[11]

Much of the work of CNAs is similar to what home care aides do. They assist in the dressing, bathing, feeding, and toileting of residents who have difficulty with ADLs, and they also play a role in monitoring for changes in residents' condition. In other respects, however, the work is different. CNAs are not isolated in homes and are supervised on a regular basis by floor nurses. They typically are responsible for multiple residents, who are often not the same people from day to day. Their work is tightly scheduled and rushed because of the nursing home routines: for example, they need to have all their charges dressed and ready for meals at fixed times. In the National Nursing Assistant Survey (NNAS), 43 percent of CNAs reported that they did not have enough time to provide residents with adequate assistance with their ADLs.[12] Christine Bishop described the work as follows:

> Nursing home direct care jobs have few skill requirements, minimal selectivity in hiring, cursory initial orientation and on-the-job training, low wages and benefits, and supervision focused on completion of defined tasks. Nursing assistants describe the work itself as repetitive, taxing, and demeaning. Workers are treated as unreliable and easily replaceable. High turnover justifies low on-the-job investment in workers' skills, because internally trained workers are likely to leave for better opportunities.[13]

Much as happens with home care aides, CNAs' work can be physically dangerous. In the NNAS, 56 percent of CNAs reported that they had been injured at work.[14] In 2004, their injury rate was three and a half times the national average for all occupations.[15]

CNAs frequently face the same lack of respect that challenges home care aides. In the NNAS, 31 percent of respondents disagreed with the statement that they were "respected at work," and another 32 percent only somewhat agreed with it.[16] Susan Eaton's fieldwork in nursing homes has revealed that about 70 percent of managers view CNAs with disdain. A manager at one of these facilities commented that

> we can't involve employees in developing systems with a customer focus. . . . The great majority of people who do nursing aide, housekeeping, laundry, and food service work are there because it is the best job they can get currently. . . . They have a low sense of self-esteem. . . . These people, not like you and me, [they] do not see life as something to take charge of. They see life as one uncontrollable event, something that happens to them. . . . You cannot walk in the door with a typical TQM project, you can't tell them to accept responsibility for the care giving system, you can't tell them to work in a quality team environment, because to do any of that requires them to take charge of their jobs. And they can't do that.[17]

There are signs of progress and improvement, and as we will see in a later chapter, there is a growing movement, often termed "culture change," to shift nursing homes in a more patient-centered direction. Efforts to more fully involve CNAs in care teams are inherent to these models, suggesting that their roles are more respected and they are treated better than in traditional nursing homes.[18] Even in these settings, however, the work remains intense, time pressures are unrelieved, and wages are still low.[19]

THE GOOD AND THE BAD: HIGH-ROAD VERSUS LOW-ROAD EMPLOYERS

In the academic and policy discussion about improving job quality and reducing the incidence of low-wage jobs, a strong theme has been the distinction between so-called high-road and low-road employers. These overly simplified terms are meant to capture the idea that some firms put a positive value on their employees' welfare and are willing to avoid squeezing them economically to maximize short-term profits. What might be termed a sub-debate in this discussion is the question of whether high-road practices are in fact profit-maximizing and in the long-run interests of shareholders. Or do such firms engage in a trade-off between profits, on the one hand, and employee welfare, on the other, because they are willing to sacrifice some of one in order to get more of the other? In this discourse, low-road employers are those that seek to get every possible ounce of low-paid work out of their workforce and see this as the road to maximum profitability.

Scholars and activists interested in this debate also have focused on ways to grow the number of high-road employers and reduce the number of low-road employers, such as through regulation, incentives, jaw-boning, demonstrations of the benefits of the high road, and unionization. With a variety of people involved in this discussion, different views about the relative efficacy of each of these strategies have naturally emerged.

If we were to characterize home care agencies along this dimension, particularly Medicaid-dependent agencies, it would be fair to say that few fall into the high-road category and that most are either somewhere in the middle or bottom feeders. But the high road does exist in the home care industry, and looking more closely at a high-road agency not only shows what is possible but also reveals the limitations of best intentions and best efforts given the existing financing and institutional structures of the industry.

The Good: Taking the High Road

Cooperative Home Care Associates (CHCA) is a medium-size agency in New York City serving about 3,000 clients (mostly in the Bronx), virtually all of whom are on Medicaid. CHCA was founded in 1985 and was explicitly intended to serve as a model for a good home health agency.[20] As such, the agency is organized to maximize the quality of the jobs—subject, of course, to the constraints of the reimbursement regime and the need to stay in business. A core feature is that CHCA is one of the largest worker-owned organizations in the nation. This organizational structure means a good deal to the employees, as illustrated by a typical comment in a conversation I had with a home care aide: "I enjoy the worker ownership of CHCA. It makes me feel [like] a partner."

In some respects, CHCA looks like all other home care agencies. An insurance company refers a client, and then, depending on the specifics of the relationship with the insurance firm, either CHCA or the insurance company assesses the case and determines a treatment plan, including the number of hours the home care aide will work. At that point, the aide goes to work. From here on, however, the CHCA model diverges from the norm.

The CHCA home care aide has had more and different training than average. Seventy-five hours of training is required by federal regulation (for home health aides), but CHCA provides nearly 140 hours. The training is employer-based—that is, it takes place at the agency rather than, for example, in a school—and it is experiential; home care aides are thus exposed to the realities of the work. I will have more to say about this training in chapter 7.

CHCA works hard to ensure that home care aides get full-time work and endeavors to piece together cases (if an assigned case is less than full-time) to ensure that this happens. For many years prior to the new federal rules on overtime, CHCA paid overtime at a rate above that required by New York State. CHCA also does its best to keep home care aides from feeling isolated and unsupported in their work with clients. Access to care managers is relatively straightforward, and in a new initiative, senior home care aides regularly visit home care aides in client homes to help with issues that might arise. All of this pays off in a much lower turnover rate at CHCA than at more typical agencies.

A visitor to CHCA sees an organization whose vibe supports these facts. Home care aides congregate in a cafeteria and chat while waiting to meet with staff or take further training. Offices are open, and care managers and care coordinators (many of whom are former home care aides) are easily accessible. The CEO's office is near the cafeteria, and he chats with home care aides over the course of the day.

CHCA is affiliated with two other organizations. PHI is the nation's leading policy shop and think tank on home health issues, and it distributes a widely respected training curriculum to other agencies and nursing homes throughout the country. It is virtually impossible to pick up a report on home health care without coming across numerous citations of PHI's research. PHI is also very active at the state level in New York and is deeply involved in a wide range of issues, including the politics of reimbursement rates and regulations regarding the scope of work of home care aides and nurses.

The third leg of the triangle is Independent Care Systems (ICS); a managed care insurance company with roots in serving the disability community, ICS also serves the elderly. ICS is known for a more generous reimbursement policy and more creative care management than is the norm in the industry.

CHCA and PHI play major roles in the national dialogue regarding home health care and, along with other agencies, are model employers. But it is important to understand that they operate within a framework that puts a ceiling on the quality of home care aide jobs. For all its good intentions and genuinely high-road practices, the wage at CHCA is still $11 an hour (plus benefits), largely owing to the funding and reimbursement constraints of Medicaid. However, and to repeat a theme that is central to the argument I develop in later chapters, CHCA's wage is also shaped by a limited vision of what home care aides can do and how they might fit into the health care system.

The Bad: Taking the Low Road

In any industry with tens of thousands of establishments, many of them small mom-and-pop organizations, it would not be surprising to find some that flout labor laws or engage in illegal behavior with respect to their clients or revenue sources. That said, there are several reasons to suspect that misbehavior is more widespread in the home health industry than average. Low-wage industries in general are more likely to be sites of misbehavior such as withholding wages or not paying overtime as required by law.[21] This happens because low-wage workers typically lack the power or representation to defend their rights under employment law, and also because they find themselves in a job market with an excess supply of people needing jobs.

The second source of concern is that, with home health agencies largely funded by public monies, the temptation must be substantial to take advantage of weak and fragmented oversight. Indeed, the CMS has a website devoted to reporting fraud, but the task is made difficult in the context of Medicaid by the diversity of state policies and oversight procedures.

Fraudulent billing does not necessarily damage employees, but the same cannot be said for the considerable fraud and abuse aimed at employees, as recently documented by the National Employment Law Project.[22] Sometimes this happens via straight-out wage theft, as documented in North Carolina by the *Raleigh News and Observer*; the newspaper's investigation also showed a pattern of firms shutting down and opening up under a new name in order to avoid enforcement.[23] Other times more subtle tactics, such as illegal misclassification, are used: in Maryland and Pennsylvania, home health agencies forced home care aides previously treated and classified as employees to sign an agreement that they were independent contractors.[24]

CONCLUSION

Home care aides and CNAs, though a diverse group, are generally committed to their clients, very constrained in what they are allowed to do, and eager to do more. It seems fair to say that they have as much impact on the quality of life of their clients as any other member of the health team, if not more. Nevertheless, they are neither viewed with respect nor rewarded fairly for their work. The remaining chapters analyze the system that generates these outcomes. But before moving on to examine the system, I want to close this chapter with the comments of a woman whose history is not typical but who has seen it all. She began her career as a home care aide, transitioned into a clerical position, and then took a managerial position in an agency before going on to do similar work in an insurance company. When I spoke with her, she was helping to manage a training program for home care aides. I asked for her opinion on the state of the home care agency. "Health care is a business," she replied,

and everybody is worried about the cost. And the aide sees all of these articles about billions of dollars in health care and looks at her little $10 an hour. And then thinks about the fact that you have to work three cases to have a forty-hour week. And how much car fare that is, how much child care that is. . . . For them, it's very difficult to think about this being a multibillion-dollar industry that can't survive without them. They know that their patient will go to the hospital if they don't come to work because she's not going to accept the replacement. And therefore, she's going to forget to take her medicine or she's going to take it twice, and she's going to be in the hospital. So they never take a day off.

CHAPTER 4

The Job Market

Someone who wants to take care of people by being a direct care worker can choose from among a variety of arrangements. The first choice is between working in a nursing home as a certified nursing assistant or working in clients' homes as a home care aide. If the choice is to be a home care aide, then the options are working for an agency, working as a self-employed independent contractor above the table, or working as a self-employed aide below the table, in the gray market. Some people choose to combine these options—for example, working for an agency but being self-employed in a second job on the side.

In part, these choices are driven by preferences. One person may prefer the structured work and colleagueship of a nursing home, while another prefers the independence and close personal relationships found in a home care setting. But often the choice is forced. Agencies frequently do not provide aides with enough hours, and so they are forced into a second job. Or the home care aide may be undocumented and so the gray market is the only choice.

The labor market for home care aides and CNAs is a complicated cross-section of these choices. It does make sense to talk of an overall labor market because the skills and demographics are broadly similar and increasingly certifications overlap. Additionally, to the extent that there is easy movement between these categories, there is one labor market. On the other hand, as we will see, there is some quality segmentation by category, as well as less mobility between CNA jobs and home care jobs than is often thought.

THE MARKET FOR HOME CARE AIDES

The labor market for CNAs is relatively straightforward since they are all "regular" employees who work for an organization, albeit one whose revenue is partly constrained by government regulation that puts a cap on CNA compensation. By contrast, the home care aide job market is more complicated, and I begin with that.

In a typical labor market, wages may be affected by rules but they can adjust to shifts in supply and demand. A ceiling is set on the wages of many home care aides, however, by the Medicaid reimbursement system. A Medicaid agency simply cannot pay more than is permitted by the reimbursement structure, which is driven by political and budgetary considerations and is only loosely affected by the supply and demand for home care aide services. Hours of work are regulated in part by the agency itself and in part by the rules of Medicaid or the managed care company that Medicaid utilizes.

By contrast, wages and hours are set by the client and the home care aide in the self-employed market. With little regulation and few institutional structures (beyond, perhaps, the registries and websites that help match home care aides with clients), this market probably most resembles the market for maids. Self-employed aides find employment via either informal networks or registries and intermediaries such as geriatric care managers. This market is lightly regulated, but it does seem probable that most of these home care aides would report themselves to the census.

Finally, some home care aides work informally under the table (or in the gray market). These aides are like self-employed home care aides in that they find work via networks, but there is no regulation of their work, and it is uncertain whether they report to the census-taker that they work as a home care aide. All observers agree that there are probably a great many gray market home care aides (ranging from an aide who does the work full-time to the neighbor down the street who earns a few extra dollars working only a few hours), but there has been little precise measurement of this market.

My estimate is that there are about 1,982,000 agency home care aides and 217,000 self-employed aides. (See appendix B for an explanation of how I derived these figures.)

An additional complication is that some home care aides move between the segments of the industry when they change jobs, with consequences for their working conditions and compensation. In the following section, I offer some ideas about how this plays out.

Home Care Aide Turnover and Commitment

If there is one labor market "indicator" that captures the attention of all interested parties—scholars, advocates, and managers alike—it is turnover. The common view is that annual turnover among home care aides is between 40 and 60 percent. An industry survey of for-profit agencies reported a median turnover rate of 61 percent, and the firms surveyed said that turnover was their biggest business challenge.[1]

Certainly, turnover can be a problem if it indicates that workers are fundamentally dissatisfied with the work. Turnover can also be a challenge because it compels employers to invest resources in seeking out new employees. And of course, turnover can reduce the quality of care. With continuity, a home care aide can learn a good deal about a client's needs and better meet them; turnover disrupts what is often a very personal relationship between a client and a home care aide.

Beyond these management and delivery issues, turnover is also a core indicator of the state of the labor market for home care aides, since it is an indirect measure of labor supply. Not surprisingly, turnover rates over time are correlated with the overall state of the economy: turnover rises during periods marked by a strong job market, and it declines as the labor market weakens.[2] Here I am more interested in what might be termed the long-term or structural nature of turnover. In this context, there are three stories we might tell about turnover.

One view is that the home care workforce is inherently unstable and exhibits low commitment to the field. A person who is a home care aide today might be just as happy being a fast-food worker tomorrow. At a simple level, this possibility can be checked by asking how the wages of home care workers compare to those of other low-wage occupations, after controlling for a range of personal characteristics. When I do this using the American Community Survey, I find that home care aides earn somewhat less than CNAs, more than food prep workers, and essentially the same as maids and waitresses.[3]

Another version of the inherent instability view is that the personal lives of home care aides make it difficult for them to be stable employees. This problem may be common among all low-wage workers who live on the edge of economic disaster, and it certainly plays a role in turnover among home care aides.

There is another version of the story, however, and this is that home care aides are committed to the occupation but tend to move between employers because of the low pay and disrespect they are often shown on the job. This version suggests that high turnover results from workers moving between agencies in search of better wages or working conditions, but not in and out of the occupation itself.

This last point is important: virtually every party to the turnover discussion is an employer bemoaning the high turnover they face. But it is certainly possible that high turnover across agencies reflects efforts by home care aides to find a better place to work and that movement in and out of the field is lower than that perceived by employers. Home care aides are paid poorly, often do not get enough hours, and are frequently isolated and treated with something bordering on contempt. It is not surprising that they move between employers seeking better conditions. Recent research points directly to the impact of working conditions on agency turnover.[4] But even if they often change employers, do home care aides stay in the field? Are they committed to their work as an occupation or profession? Making these distinctions is important to the question of whether investments in the skills and training of home care sides will have a long-run payoff for the health care system.

I begin by looking at commitment to the field. I then ask about the relationship of turnover to wages and working conditions before turning to the issue of movement across different segments of the job market and the question of quality segmentation.

Home Care Aides' Commitment to the Field

Whether home care aides are committed to working in their field is a hard question to answer because longitudinal data on home care aides are scarce. One clue comes from a survey of agency-based home care aides that the federal government conducted in 2007.[5] The paradox of turnover is apparent in these data. On the one hand, 70 percent of home care aides reported that they had been working as a home care aide for six or more years, and 50 percent had been working in the field for eleven or more years. On the other hand, over one-third said that they were likely to leave their current job within a year, and 45 percent reported holding two or more jobs in the previous year. These data suggest that home care aides are considerably more committed to the field than to any particular employer. However, the survey had a small sample size, it was limited to agency home care aides, and it is nearly a decade old.

No longitudinal labor force survey has been conducted that includes enough home care aides to permit analysis. Over a short time span, however, the cross-sectional Current Population Survey (CPS) can be utilized to study mobility because of its unique design: the same respondents are included in the survey for four months in a row. Using a complex method, it is possible to match people across these four months and track with considerable accuracy their mobility in and out of specific occupations. (See appendix C for a detailed explanation of how this is done.) Using this technique, I can report the fraction of people working as home care aides in month 1 who continued to work as home care aides (or, alternatively, in health care more generally) in month 4.

If we limit ourselves to the first years after the Great Recession, 2010 to 2014, then 78 percent of home care aides in month 1 were still working as home care aides four months later. A naive extrapolation leads to an annual turnover rate of 53 percent, which is high, and also consistent with conventional wisdom. However, this extrapolation is naive because it is the turnover-prone home care aides who are most likely to leave quickly, in the first four months; the subsequent two four-month periods will witness lower turnover rates. When I make an adjustment to account for this, I estimate a turnover rate of 43 percent, which is notably lower, albeit still high.

An additional adjustment is to ask where home care aides go when they leave that occupation. In fact, half of those who leave the field are leaving the labor force, but half continue working in another occupation. Of those in another occupation, many enter another health care job—for example, as a CNA or hospital aide, or even as a nurse (since a nontrivial number of home care aides are nurses working part-time in a second job to support themselves). If we do not count as turnover the people who stay in health care (because they remain committed to the health care field), the annual turnover rate is reduced to 32 percent.

These revised turnover rates are important because they demonstrate that the commitment of home care aides to their field is stronger than it appears if we were to just look at their commitment to their employer.

THE MARKET FOR CERTIFIED NURSING ASSISTANTS

The work of CNAs and home care aides is similar in many respects, and demographically those who take these jobs are virtually identical, with home care aides somewhat more likely to be immigrants. We would expect their demographic similarities to imply similar labor market circumstances, but in fact there are some important distinctions between the two kinds of direct care workers.

First, there are differences, though subtle ones, in training requirements: the federal regulations require that CNAs and one subset of home care aides, home health aides, have seventy-five hours of training. However, states are more likely to require CNAs than home health aides to have augmented hours of training, and for another subset of home care aides, personal care assistants, there is no federal training standard and states are very uneven in whether they require any training at all.

A second difference is that while many aspects of the work are similar, the fact that CNAs are employed in bureaucratic institutions with close supervision and a range of rules and procedures implies that the preferences—and to some extent the personalities—of those who take these jobs may differ. Finally, the institutional structures of the labor markets differ. There is no gray market for CNAs, nor is there a private-pay market. This has implications for turnover rates as well as for opportunities for quality segmentation.

We have seen that CNAs earn more than home care aides ($20,025 median annual earnings in 2015 compared to $15,019, and they are slightly more likely to work full-time). That said, CNAs are hardly well off: their earnings are still low and in fact have declined in recent years.

It is difficult to parse out just why CNAs earn more, but several possibilities arose in my conversations with those in the field. First, as just noted, the human capital of CNAs may on average be deeper than that of home care aides. Second, agencies that hire home care aides make money by a simple markup of their wages, whereas CNA compensation is buried in the overall reimbursement that nursing homes receive per resident. As a consequence, there is more margin for small wage increases in CNA compensation. Also, nursing home lobbies are more powerful at the state level than home health agencies. Finally, unionization came to nursing homes before home care, and so there may have been a legacy effect of higher wages.

A reasonable question is whether CNA turnover patterns are similar to those of home care aides. The compensation may be slightly better, but CNAs still earn a low wage and work a very difficult job. Deploying the census turnover data for CNAs as I did for aides, I find that CNAs have slightly lower turnover and are slightly more committed to the job market than home care aides. Whereas 78 percent of home care aides in month 1 were working as home care aides in month 4, the figure for CNAs is 81 percent. And overall, 94 percent of CNAs in month 1 were working in any job four months later compared to 89 percent of home care aides.

With these considerations in mind, the obvious question is whether the labor market for CNAs and home care aides is essentially unitary or whether these in fact represent different markets. Certainly, there are overlaps, but there are also reasons to think that the markets are different. Although there is overlap in training, the overlap is not complete, and in most states CNAs and home care aides have two different certifications (and of course personal care assistants may have no certification at all). Another difference that may seem prosaic but in fact is important to the people involved is that in most parts of the country home care aides need to have a car or access to easy transportation because their work involves moving between locations, whereas CNAs typically work in one workplace. Finally, preferences matter: CNAs work in bureaucratic settings with close supervision, while home care aides do not.

What do the data show? If we look at the CPS and ask, as I have just described, what fraction of people who in month 1 were CNAs were home care aides in month 4, the figure is 3.4 percent. And if we ask what fraction of home care aides in month 1 became CNAs in month 4, the answer is 2.4 percent. Summing the two, just under 6 percent of people moved between the occupations over a four-month period. A naive extrapolation would be that 18 percent move over a year, although, as discussed, this figure would be too high because of the "movement-prone" who show up first in the data. In short, there is certainly interaction between the two markets, but at the same time they are far from being unified.

TURNOVER, WAGES, AND
WORKING CONDITIONS

Absent a careful experiment, we cannot definitively apportion the share of turnover that is attributable to the "character" of the workforce versus the conditions of their work. But an array of evidence suggests that the conditions of work do play an important role. Two national demonstrations have aimed at reducing turnover—the Robert Wood Johnson Foundation Better Jobs Better Care (BJBC) program and the Demonstration to Improve the Direct Service Community Workforce, supported by federal funding. Both efforts were the subject of serious evaluations.[6] But remarkably, in neither demonstration were wages increased, in neither were career ladders created, in neither was the job of home care aides enlarged in any significant way, and in neither were there any measures of client outcomes. Instead, the demonstrations focused on recruitment, marketing, selection, and improving the quality of supervision in the direction of "kinder more gentle" management. In the BJBC demonstration, there was no impact on turnover or job satisfaction, while in the Direct Service Community Workforce demonstration improvements in recruiting (such as more realistic job previews) did reduce turnover.

In thinking about what these demonstrations did and did not attempt to do, it is easy to be critical, but this would be unfair. Reading between the lines of the reports, we can see that the extremely decentralized, indeed disorganized, system of long-term care provision, with its multiple actors and conflicting interests, made it very difficult to test innovations at scale and with any degree of uniformity across sites.

There is more recent evidence that improvements in selection and enhanced training can reduce turnover. As already noted, turnover at a high-road agency, Cooperative Home Care Associates, is well below the average in New York City, although, with wages mandated by law to be equalized across agencies in the city, CHCA wages are no higher than average.[7] Another strand of evidence comes from a sizable demonstration at three New York agencies that combined a more careful selection process with enhanced training and peer mentoring and coaching for supervisors. Turnover fell very substantially, although the design of the intervention made it difficult to parse out the contribution of the various elements of the program.[8]

But what about wages? Would turnover fall if wages were improved? There is scattered evidence that this is true. In the early 1990s, a four-city demonstration sponsored by the Ford Foundation and New York City showed that increases in wages led to very substantial reductions in turnover.[9] This finding is reinforced by more recent research in California that showed that home care aide turnover fell in response to wage increases due to living wage ordinances.[10] In Wyoming, between 2001 and 2004, the legislature raised total compensation for home care aides in the developmentally disabled home care program from $9.08 an hour to $13.19 an hour, and during that period turnover fell from 52 percent to 32 percent.[11] A similar pattern emerged in North Dakota between 2002 and 2010, when reductions in annual turnover rates coincided with legislative increases in compensation for home care aides.[12]

Finally, with respect to CNAs, a survey of over two hundred aides in Massachusetts nursing homes found that higher wages and good basic supervision (notably, being treated with respect and provided with feedback and assistance) were both associated with reduced turnover intentions.[13]

WAGES AND QUALITY SEGMENTATION

If home care aides can move between working for agencies and working as independent contractors, how might we expect this to play out? Wages and working conditions in the agency segment are capped, while it is possible to earn more in the self-employed private-pay market. In the American Community Survey, the median earnings of self-employed home care aides are $3,000 a year more than earnings for other home care aides, and this difference is not due to hours of work: self-employed home care aides are actually less likely to work full-time and full-year than other home care aides (table 4.1). Clearly, then, a good many home care aides are in the self-employed sector earning higher wages.

However, there is a risk associated with moving into the self-employed segment: the uncertainty of finding work. Considering these two offsetting features together—potentially higher wages but also greater risk—suggests that it is the most qualified home care aides who move into self-employment. That is to say, there may be quality segmentation.

This possibility was sharply confirmed in my conversations with senior leaders in two very progressive home health organizations. Although each

Table 4.1   Earnings Distribution of Home Care Aides by
              Employment Status, 2015

	Not Self-Employed	Self-Employed
Twenty-fifty percentile	$9,011	$8,411
Median	15,019	18,023
Seventy-fifty percentile	23,630	26,333
Ninetieth percentile	41,552	46,058

Source: 2015 ACS.

Table 4.2   Characteristics of Home Care Aides by Employment
              Status, 2015

	Not Self-Employed	Self-Employed
Full-time, full-year	40.9%	34.7%
Less than high school	18.9	16.7
Any college	46.3	50.7
Immigrant	27.4	24.1
Poor English	21.1	19.7
Ages eighteen to twenty-four	28.2	15.1

Source: 2015 ACS.

obviously had access to agency home care aides and probably could have selected the aide they wished to employ, given their senior position, both went into the self-employment market to find help for their own mothers. When I pressed them for an explanation, they offered two reasons: they thought that at the margin the private-pay home care aides were better, and more importantly, these aides were free of the scope of practice restrictions that hobble agency home care aides.

The data do show human capital differences: self-employed home care aides are more likely than non-self-employed home care aides to have some college, and a smaller proportion of self-employed home care aides are high school dropouts and hence may be more skilled and experienced. Self-employed home care aides are also notably older than other aides. All this said, the differences are not huge: for example, 17 percent of self-employed home care aides are high school dropouts compared to 19 percent of other aides (table 4.2).

CONCLUSION

The job market for home care aides is fractured. For those employed in the Medicaid world, compensation and hours are determined by bureaucratic rules, whereas for independent contractors, whether they work above or below the table, the market is more flexible. Because people can move back and forth between these segments, there tends to be something of a quality divide, with the better-qualified home care aides working on their own. But importantly, for neither group is compensation decent, and both groups face the challenges of being disrespected and confined to a limited role in the care system. Contrary to much discussion, home care aides are broadly committed to their occupation. High turnover rates reflect not lack of commitment but low compensation: people move between agencies to find slightly better-paying work. But home care aides are generally committed to the occupation. There is some evidence that improvement in compensation reduces turnover, both between employers and in and out of the occupation itself.

Given this complex market, how can we move forward to improve opportunities for home care aides? Any strategy must, in my view, be based in large part on enlarging their scope of practice so that enhanced productivity can justify improved compensation. But this raises the question of whether in fact home care aides can do more, and whether there is evidence that extending their scope of practice will result in a payoff to the system. I turn to this question in part II, but before taking it up, I discuss family caregivers and consumer-directed care—a system that is an important alternative to agency-based care delivery.

CHAPTER 5

Family Caregivers and Consumer-Directed Programs

As we have seen, family caregivers provide a great deal of help and are, in fact, the dominant source of support for both younger and older disabled people. These caregivers are often unpaid and, unfortunately, often unsupported. Family caregivers are also deeply involved in an important variant of paid care, so-called consumer-directed programs, a model in which "consumers"—those in need of care—avoid agencies and directly hire their caregivers. Family members provide roughly 70 percent of the paid care under this model.

FAMILY CAREGIVERS

The amount of help provided by family caregivers dwarfs the proportion provided by paid home care aides, and the vast majority are unpaid and offer their support out of love. It must be acknowledged, however, that many provide this care because they cannot afford paid help. Additionally, some family caregivers are paid and compensated via the consumer-directed variant of Medicaid.

A fundamental objective of any effort to improve our system of long-term care must be to support all of these family caregivers and ameliorate the consequences for them with respect to their own physical and mental health and their opportunities in the job market. As we will see, we also need to understand going forward that the pool of potential family caregivers is expected to shrink relative to the universe of need.

How Many Family Caregivers Are There?

There is general agreement that family caregivers number in the many millions and that they represent the majority of caregivers, but precise figures are hard to come by and estimates vary. The AARP recently conducted a nationally representative survey and concluded that over 43 million adults serve as unpaid caregivers. The Council of Economic Advisers arrived at a very similar figure, and the Institute of Medicine put the number at between 29 million and 52 million.[1] The 2011 National Study of Caregiving put the figure close to 18 million, as did the Institute of Medicine in a report that was limited to care for older adults.[2] My own estimate, the basis of which is explained in appendix B, is just over 20.6 million.

What Do Family Caregivers Do?

According to the National Study of Caregiving, 21 percent of family caregivers are spouses, 29 percent are daughters, 18 percent are sons, and 22 percent are other relatives. Two-thirds of these caregivers help their family member with self-care and mobility, nearly all do household chores, three-quarters help with interactions with the health care system, and just over half assist with medical tasks.[3] If we limit ourselves to caregiving for people ages sixty-five and older, 15 percent of family caregivers are in that role for a year or less, 15 percent are in it for more than ten years, and the remainder fall between these extremes.[4] Common sense suggests that the presence of a family caregiver is likely to have a positive effect on the well-being of people in need of assistance, and the literature supports this expectation.[5]

As is the case for professional home care aides, family caregivers often feel isolated. In the AARP survey, only one-third of the family caregivers reported having had a conversation with a member of the medical or social work team about what was needed to care for the family member. And also like paid home care aides, family caregivers evidently are not considered part of the care team. Only 39 percent reported to the AARP that they had received any visits from health care professionals, and nearly half reported that they had received no training in wound care, which they felt was the most difficult task they faced.[6] Despite this lack of training and their isolation, there is evidence, based on random assignment, that outcomes are better when family caregivers are part of the care team.[7]

A summary of the situation facing family caregivers was provided recently by the Institute of Medicine; remarkably, it sounds in many respects much like a summary of the situation of paid caregivers:

> Despite the integral role that family caregivers play in the care of older adults with disabilities and complex health needs, they are often marginalized or ignored in the delivery of health care and LTSS, and are often ignored in public policy as well. Paradoxically, family caregivers may be excluded from treatment decisions and care planning while the providers who exclude them assume their availability to perform the wide range of tasks prescribed by the older adults' care plan.[8]

Hours of Work

We cannot measure the emotional intensity of caregiving work, a factor that is particularly important for family members. But it is helpful to ask about the number of hours family and friends spend on this work. Census data shed no light on this question because they cannot identify unpaid family and friends, but the Health and Retirement Survey does collect data on up to eight "helpers" per respondent, and for each helper it asks whether the person was paid and the days and hours per day that the person typically worked. Keeping in mind that these data are limited to recipients who are ages fifty or older, we can get a useful sense of the intensity of the work. In the HRS, only 7 percent of the 15.3 million family or friend caregivers were paid, and the remainder were unpaid. Figure 5.1 provides these data for unpaid family and friends.

Before I discuss these patterns, it is worth repeating a central point: These data capture the hours that people spend providing care. They do not measure in any way the emotional intensity or other challenges involved in the work. Nor do they capture the amount of time caregivers spend in planning, arranging for care, and so on. Hence, even if only a few hours of the time they spend caring for their family member are measurable, most of these caregivers

Figure 5.1   Distribution of Hours Spent on Caregiving Work by
              Unpaid Family Members, 2012

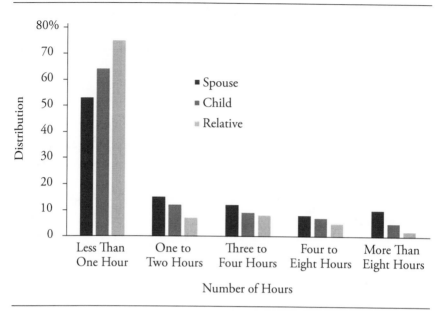

Source: 2012 HRS.
Note: Data refer to consumers age fifty or older.

bring considerable effort and commitment to this work and experience significant strain.

It is clear that the majority of unpaid family members work relatively few
hours: over half of both those who are paid and those who are unpaid worked
two or fewer hours per day. Although there is no way of knowing from the
HRS, it is certainly possible that many of these caregivers helped in the
morning, went off to work, and then returned in the evening to help again.
The flip side of the data is that, while they are in the minority, a nontrivial
percentage of family members did provide care for a considerable number of
hours every day.

Consequences of Family Caregiving

We saw that paid home care aides fare very poorly in the labor market. What
about family caretakers? Over half of employed family caregivers reported

that they had to make a change in their work—for example, reducing their hours or taking a leave of absence. Does family caregiving adversely affect their economic prospects? In one study, MetLife estimated a lifetime cost of more than $200,000 for men and women (with women losing more than men).[9] However, estimates along these lines are naive, because they fail to control for the possibility that people who choose to provide unpaid caregiving would not otherwise work or have worse earnings prospects than those who do not offer themselves for caregiving.

Controlling for this possibility is challenging, but a recent careful effort managed to do so in its examination of adult children (average age fifty-five) who cared for parents or parents-in-law.[10] The researchers found that men who provided care were 2.4 percentage points less likely to work than those who did not, and that women caregivers worked somewhere between three and ten hours a week less than other women and suffered an earnings penalty of 3 percent. All this adds up to a nontrivial cost to unpaid family caregivers. There is also extensive research showing that family caregiving has adverse health consequences for the caregiver.[11]

CONSUMER-DIRECTED CARE

In most parts of the country, the agency model seems the obvious and natural approach to long-term care. People who need assistance call an agency, which then sends one of its employees, a home care aide, to help them. How this care is reimbursed varies, but the point is that an agency is the organization that employs, trains, and supervises home care aides.

However, the universe of organized paid help also includes another model: people receiving Medicaid support hire their own home care aides, with agencies playing no role in how this is managed. This model, called consumer-directed (sometimes participant-directed) care, is important because of its merits and because its advocates are significant political players when it comes to long-term care.

In the generic version of consumer-directed care, because clients (Medicaid beneficiaries) hire (and fire) their own home care aides and are responsible for supervision, they are in charge of their own care. The home care aide is seen as an extension of the client, and thus scope of practice regulations and the restrictions of state nurse practice acts do not apply; the home care aide can do anything the client desires. Depending on the rules of the state, the client may also handle the budget and payroll (perhaps with the assistance of a payroll processing organization); if not, the state pays the home care aide selected by the client.

This model has achieved substantial penetration. A consumer-directed option is available in every state's Medicaid program, and in 2013, 838,000 clients across the country were in such programs (out of 3.2 million in all Medicaid home and community-based programs).[12] This said, the penetration of consumer-directed programs varies considerably. Home care in California, Washington, and Oregon is overwhelmingly consumer-directed (for Medicaid); of the 838,000 clients cared for through this option, half a million are in California along with another 100,000 or so in the states of Washington and Oregon combined. For every 1,000 disabled adults in California, 127 are in consumer-directed programs; by contrast, the number is 4.6 in Illinois, 8.8 in New Jersey, 58.0 in Washington State, 1.9 in Georgia, 78.0 in Vermont, and 1.0 in Alabama.[13]

Consumer-directed programs are often linked to the concerns of the disability community because they originated, at least in part, in the political activism of disability advocates, who continue to protect the model and push for its expansion. Many in the disability community, particularly younger people, are understandably insistent on maintaining the maximum possible control over their lives. As one person with a physical disability commented in a conference I attended, "The most important thing for me is to control who walks in my door."

That said, it is important to recognize that disability concerns and consumer-directed care are not fully synonymous. The most central disability concern is the adequate implementation of the *Olmstead* decision, which requires maximum possible community integration. This can be achieved via agency models as well as through consumer-directed programs. Consumer-directed programs are also relevant to some elderly clients. It is notable that in California about 60 percent of those served are elderly.[14] Whether the model makes sense for cognitively challenged elderly clients is an open question, although advocates point out that a client can appoint someone to help manage the care.

An important feature of the consumer-directed model (though not a requirement) is that paid family labor is dominant, and this certainly helps explain its support. There is some dispute about why most consumer-directed home care aides are family or friends (but not spouses, which is prohibited in most states). Some argue that the reliance on family and friends flows from the underfunding of programs, which makes it difficult to hire competent nonrelative home care aides. Others argue that clients themselves are likely to prefer being cared for by someone with whom they feel most comfortable. And family members get paid for what they would often be doing regardless. In any case, family members are central to the program. In California, 73 percent of home care aides are related to the client, and most of the rest are friends.[15] Although data are scarce, my conversations with people in Washington State supported this figure. A survey in Massachusetts found that only 32 percent of home care aides in the consumer-directed program were strangers to the client.[16]

The consumer-directed model has strong intuitive appeal. Imagine that you become disabled, whether because of an accident or simply as a result of aging. Assuming that you maintain your cognitive capacity, it would not be surprising if you were to prefer choosing and supervising your home care aide rather than have an agency send you someone over whom you have little control. But this simple scenario leaves open a number of questions. What if you are cognitively diminished? Does the model still make sense? Are you open to the hassle of finding a home care aide if no family member is willing and ready to take on this job? Does the home care aide get trained, and if so, by whom? In the absence of an agency, what happens if the home care aide does not show up for work and you therefore cannot get out of bed? Consumer-directed programs offer answers to these questions, but at the same time these issues also point to potential worries about the general applicability of the model, which I discuss in greater detail later in the chapter.

The Growth of Consumer-Directed Care

Like every movement, consumer-directed care has its founding myth. There is general agreement that it began on the West Coast, but after that narratives diverge. In one version of the founding story, the model emerged in California when a group of polio patients in Los Angeles County living in a rehabilitation hospital pushed for more independence and state officials addressing this concern realized that these patients could be treated more cheaply at home.[17] Another version emphasizes the activism of disabled students at the University of California at Berkeley.[18] Yet another founding story points to Oregon, the first state in the country to apply for a Medicaid waiver to permit expenditures on home and community-based care (instead of nursing homes); Oregon also innovated with what was termed the client-employed provider model.

Advocates and clients had strong feelings about this movement. In the words of one advocate: "The disability community has not had good experiences with agencies that provide personal attendant services. Traditional home health agencies use a medical focus and tend to want to control what goes [on] in the home of the service recipients."[19] A client was eloquent on the subject of self-direction:

> My disability is limiting physically, yet . . . I have become a truly empowered person. Most able-bodied individuals cannot understand the importance of having choice and control in their daily lives. Waking up and facing daily decisions of what foods to eat, what clothes to wear, and whether I should shower or take a bath are freedoms that are inherent in most lives. With the Personal Preference Program, I have been granted total choice and control over my personal care needs. I think this program is great. Every consumer needs self-direction.[20]

A key event in the national acceptance of consumer-directed care was the Cash and Counseling Demonstration, which began enrollment in Arkansas, Florida, and New Jersey between 1998 and 2000 and ended enrollment in 2002. The demonstration, funded by the Robert Wood Johnson Foundation and carefully evaluated by Mathematica, was structured as a horse race between traditional agency services and the consumer-directed model (called Cash and Counseling). Unlike virtually any other program innovation in home and community-based care, this was a large-scale, well-executed random assignment evaluation, albeit with one crucial and potentially problematic feature: instead of randomly assigning long-term care clients to the evaluation, clients volunteered to enter the demonstration, and it was among this group that the random assignment between Cash and Counseling and agencies was implemented. I discuss momentarily the implications of this widely overlooked feature.

The demonstration offered budget authority to participants—in effect, they had a voucher with which to hire home care aides and purchase other services—and the results were broadly positive. Generalizing across the three states, the treatment group was more likely to receive paid help than the control group (although the treatment group also received fewer total hours of care, evidently owing to a cutback in unpaid assistance); the treatment group was far more satisfied than the control group with their care and the quality of their lives; and adverse incidents occurred no more often for the treatment group than for the control group. Costs were higher for the treatment group—in large measure, however, because the controls ended up not receiving the services to which they were entitled.

These results are seen by consumer-directed care advocates as evidence that their preferred model is superior to agencies. But this is a misreading. Many in the control group actually did not receive services (for unclear reasons that may include administrative failures in the states' agency systems), and so the satisfaction measures in part end up comparing people who got services with people who did not. More seriously, selection into the demonstration itself was biased: people volunteered themselves into the overall demonstration, and it seems reasonable to think that these were people who were dissatisfied with agencies to begin with. (After all, why would someone who had a good situation with an agency give it up to enter the demonstration?) For these reasons, Cash and Counseling was not a fair horse race.

Nevertheless, the demonstration did show something of real importance: Cash and Counseling (and by extension consumer-directed care) delivered services safely, and participants had good outcomes and were satisfied. We do not know from this demonstration whether consumer-directed care is a better model than agencies, but we do know that for the population interested in having more independence, it is an effective model that safely delivers what it promises.

How Consumer-Directed Care Works

There are two basic consumer-directed models. Under so-called employer authority, the client can hire, supervise, and dismiss a home care aide. Under budget authority models, the client has hiring, firing, and supervisory power and is also given what is in effect a voucher that can be used for the home care

Figure 5.2   Distribution of Hours Spent on Caregiving Work by Paid Family Members, 2012

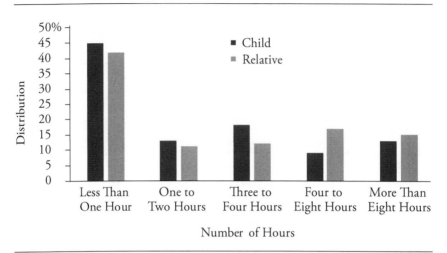

Source: 2012 HRS.
Note: Data refer to consumers age fifty or older.

aide as well as for other goods and services related to care. Most programs require background checks of home care aides, a backup plan in the event that a home care aide does not show up, and some level of case management. In addition, a client can typically designate someone to act as a representative if that becomes necessary. But mentioning these features buries the headline. As I noted earlier, a core feature of consumer-directed care is that most home care aides hired under this model are family members or friends of the client. That said, if the client does not hire a family or friend, then many states provide assistance via registries of home care aides.

The Health and Retirement Survey enables us to look at the hours of paid family members (see figure 5.2). We cannot be sure that all of these caregivers are consumer-directed aides, since the survey does not ask this question and it is possible that some are paid out of pocket (but probably not by insurance, since most insurance companies require that an aide be certified). Note also that spouses are not shown in the figure: the fact that very few spouses reported providing paid care makes sense, since virtually all states prohibit spouses from receiving compensation under consumer-directed programs.

Like family members providing unpaid care, the bulk of these paid family caregivers worked relatively few hours. And as I emphasized earlier, these data capture neither the degree of emotional commitment nor the amount of time spent organizing and planning. That said, the data do suggest that many paid family caregivers are able to hold down another job.

A second central feature of consumer-directed programs is that scope of practice laws and NPA limitations do not apply because the home care aides are seen as extensions of the clients, who can, of course, do anything they want for themselves. It is worth noting in this context that there is no evidence that clients in consumer-directed programs fare any worse than agency clients with respect to their health outcomes, raising questions about the relevance of scope of practice restrictions.

The absence of scope of practice limitations does point to a controversial question regarding consumer-directed home care aides: whether states should impose training standards, as some do for agency home care aides. Elements of the disability community oppose training standards on the principle that they would interfere with client control and "medicalize" the system. In California, this viewpoint has been dominant to the point that efforts to apply for training demonstration grants have been blocked. In Massachusetts, the state council that manages the program has refused to implement mandatory training, and even the short three-hour orientation that it does require must be provided by the client, not by a professional. By contrast, in Washington State, where home care is also predominantly consumer-directed, voters approved a referendum establishing a training requirement. A recent survey of consumer-directed programs (not weighted by number of clients) found that over half required some level of training.[21]

A final important point is that many states with consumer-directed programs have set up a state-level authority to act as a co-employer and bargain with unions about wages, though clients still do the hiring and firing and supervision. Unions advocated for the authority model in order to ease the task of organizing the thousands of home care aides working in clients' homes. Home care aides needed to vote for this model at the time the authorities were established, but subsequently the processes for joining and paying dues became automatic. Establishing these authorities was a major achievement of the union movement, and it substantially increased union density and led to significant wage improvements. That said, the future of this structure is very much in doubt owing to a recent Supreme Court decision, which I discuss in more detail later.

Tensions and Concerns

On its face, consumer-directed care is an appealing strategy. It is easy to intuit that many, if not most, people would want to control who comes to their home to care for them. Nonetheless, consumer-directed care has not expanded at the rate we would expect: the best available national survey reported that nationally, between 2010 and 2013, only 90,000 new clients enrolled in consumer-directed care.[22] Other observers agree that expansion has been slow. The most commonly offered explanation is that insurance companies, which increasingly manage state Medicaid programs, are uncomfortable with the model and discourage clients from taking it up. But other concerns about the consumer-directed model should also be considered.

Employee Welfare   It might seem natural to dismiss worries about the welfare of home care aides in consumer-directed programs on the grounds that they are family members and hence there is a unity of interest in this case between the employer (the client) and the employee. However, this easy dismissal would be a misreading of the evidence. It is important to recall that roughly 30 percent of home care aides in consumer-directed programs are neither family nor friends, and that even a good many home care aides who are family members have an interest in continuing in health care employment.

The findings from a survey conducted in California in the mid-2000s suggest that career concerns might be more salient than appears at first sight.[23] Among a small sample (383 people) of home care aides who had worked in the early 2000s and were no longer working for the same client at the time of the survey, 47 percent were still in the health care field caring for another elderly or disabled person. This rate is lower than the rate for the typical agency or professional home care aide, but it does imply that a nontrivial proportion of consumer-directed home care aides continue this kind of work. The home care aides who continued were less educated than home care aides who left the field, they were less likely to be related to their former client, and they had earned a lower hourly wage prior to their care work than those who left the field. (A Washington State survey of consumer-directed home care aides showed a similar pattern.)[24]

Additionally, a survey of consumer-directed home care aides in Massachusetts found that 67 percent were related to their client but that one-third had a prior job as a home care aide and nearly 80 percent had some prior medical experience.[25] Taken as a whole, these data reinforce the California survey and suggest that consumer-directed aides need to be taken seriously as employees.

The tensions regarding the welfare of these aides arise from two main flashpoints: wages and employment standards, and training.

Certainly, consumer-directed home care aides are likely to be responsive to wage levels; indeed, Candace Howe has shown that turnover rates of California home care aides vary with compensation levels.[26] Moreover, clashes around wages and employment standards have a long pedigree: Boris and Klein report that the young disabled Berkeley students who so effectively pushed for the consumer-directed model in the mid-1970s were more than a little ambivalent about how generous they should be regarding compensation. "A conflict of interest existed between attendants and those they served. To better stretch assistance checks, some advocates offered strategies to avoid paying social security of attendants. . . . Higher wages and benefits would balloon costs."[27]

More recently, disabled consumer-directed advocates opposed the extension of the Fair Labor Standards Act to home care aides, which would require that home care aides be paid at least the federal minimum wage as well as time and a half for overtime, and also that they be compensated for travel time. In chapter 8, I offer a more sympathetic interpretation of this opposition (on the grounds that the Department of Labor, as well as some advocates, fundamentally misunderstood the nature of consumer-directed programs), but here it is worth noting that at least one reason for their opposition was simple distributional concerns: if more resources went to home care aides, then less would go to clients to get additional hours of help.

Training, the other flashpoint for tensions surrounding employee welfare, has obvious implications for the welfare and safety of clients. Consumer-directed advocates and many advocates in the disability community oppose any effort to increase training standards for consumer-directed home care aides. As one member of the community said, "We want to take control over services. We think there has to be oversight, but we don't want someone to have to go through some kind of training that . . . [the government] comes up with. And then they're coming and working at my home, and I have to untrain them to do it the way that I want it. I know my needs best. I should be the one paying for that, doing the training." Another underlying concern may be that for family members who volunteer for this work, even though they are being paid, the time spent in training is one bridge too far.

This opposition to training runs counter to two equally reasonable perspectives. One is the public interest in ensuring that home care aides are competent to care for their clients. The client, of course, certainly cares about this too, but it does not necessarily follow that it is always appropriate for the client to be the sole judge of competence. The other perspective argues for the long-term well-being of home care aides: their compensation and future labor market opportunities may be enhanced if they have the opportunity for training.

The struggle over training has played out differently in different consumer-directed states. In California, there is no training requirement and the disability community has succeeded in blocking legislative applications for training funds from the federal government. The Kaiser Family Foundation recently reported on widespread concerns about the safety implications of the absence of training and, in support of these worries, offered data and examples of clients who suffered serious health issues because their caregivers had not received training.[28]

In contrast to California, Washington State overcame some opposition and passed a ballot initiative (actually two ballot initiatives) that led to training requirements that are essentially equivalent to those for home care aides in New York and several other states. But in Massachusetts, as in California, there is no required training for consumer-directed home aides.

Fraud and Abuse   Fraud is one of the more straightforward concerns about the consumer-directed model. The issue here is that, absent an agency, the consumer-directed model opens the door for various scams. A relative might take advantage of an older person, sign him or her up for consumer-directed care, accept compensation, and not provide good care. Or the client and the home care aide might conspire to pay the home care aide for work not done and share the illicit gains.

A second concern is not financial fraud but simple abuse: absent supervision, caregivers may abuse clients in various ways ranging from simple lack of care to theft to more serious physical violence.

I know of no systematic data on these issues. Home care aides and clients in consumer-directed models probably do receive less oversight than is the case in agency systems (although even in agency systems the degree of support and oversight is light-years away from optimal). Indeed, my conversations with observers suggest that there are good reasons to worry, and there are in fact reports of serious problems.[29] On the other hand, these concerns are not inherent in the model (see, for example, the good results in the Cash and Counseling demonstration). The solution is to invest in supports and provide case managers (and all states do have case managers) with sufficient time and support to do an adequate job of monitoring clients and their well-being.

Ease of Use   Finally, it is of course true that consumer-directed programs are not for everyone. Cognitively challenged people cannot manage their own situation, and unless they have a capable and willing relative or friend, the model seems inappropriate for them. More generally, many people may simply not want to put the time and energy into hiring, training, and supervising their own home care aide, or they may not have confidence in the backup plan if one day something should go wrong with their home care aide. For these people, the agency model makes more sense.

CONCLUSION

The consumer-directed model of home care is an important mechanism for providing caregiving and certainly should be available to those who want it and are capable of managing its complexities. For this reason, the slow diffusion of the program is troubling, and it may be important to educate insurers more extensively than has been done so far. But from our viewpoint focused on the welfare of aides, a different set of issues is raised by the program.

As is true for all home care aides, one central concern lies in compensation levels. The main consumer-directed states are unionized, but there is considerable variation in the hourly rate paid—from a relatively good rate in Washington to a less satisfactory rate in California. (I discuss this issue further when I take up the role of unions.) Besides concerns about wages, there is a hard set of concerns about training; given that many consumer-directed aides intend to remain in the health care field, the lack of training in some states is troubling. Finally, conflicts around training and compensation (notably overtime) have driven a wedge between groups that normally would be allies on long-term care policy. I take up this issue several times in the chapters that follow.

PART II

Moving the Needle

CHAPTER 6

Introduction to Part II

In the first chapter, I laid out a vision for long-term care. At the core was the creation of health teams that include home care aides. These teams would work to help people stay in their homes and communities and be as self-sufficient and independent as possible. Medical care would certainly be a part of the team's work, but this would not be a "medicalized" program but rather a holistic one, in the best sense of that word.

This vision implies that we need to reconceive the role of home care aides, and to do so we must link aides to new ideas regarding health care delivery that have gained, and continue to gain, a great deal of currency. Central to these new models are teams, health coaching, and improved transitions. In addition, home care aides should be able to assist other health providers, such as physical therapists, and in this way play a more valuable and potentially reimbursable role in the system.

Part II begins by asking about the evidence that home care aides can really do more. Would changing their role make any difference? Many of the people whom I interviewed believed that it would be possible to expand scope of practice for home care aides; in one typical comment, a senior leader in a huge agency said, "There are many smart home care aides who work as home care aides either because they like the work or because life didn't give them other opportunities. . . . I totally believe the home care aides make the difference for patients, and they have not had the opportunity to show it."

But some in the field are skeptical. The head of a progressive managed care organization, the person who hired private-pay home care aides for his mother instead of an aide from an agency he funded, scoffed at the idea that home care aides could fill a substantially expanded role. In a similar vein, a senior policymaker in the U.S. Department of Health and Human Services, the agency that oversees most national spending on long-term care, asked:

> Why should anyone expect that having a home care aide help with feeding, dressing, transferring, toileting, etc., would lead to increased ability to perform such tasks independently? . . . [Also consider] the dangers of poorly educated people who have been raised by poorly educated, dysfunctional parents taking care of vulnerable people with disabilities, especially if those clients have behavior problems. What if they were raised by parents who beat them when they were "bad"?

As I have repeatedly argued, these attitudes are widely shared and a major obstacle to progress.

Recall that about half of home care aides have at least some college education. And of course, keep in mind that many people without college education are capable and committed. Moreover, there is no evidence that clients in consumer-directed programs, which have no scope of practice limitations, have worse outcomes than clients served by agencies. These points suggest strongly that the core idea is plausible, but is there any direct evidence, and if so, what is it? This is the topic of chapter 7.

The material in chapter 7 draws from a powerful analogy. Early in the 1970s, the American automobile industry was on top of the world. The "Big Three" automakers dominated the market and were seemingly invincible. In the classic Detroit production system, frontline workers were human machines who endlessly performed repetitive tasks, were assumed to have nothing to contribute to the design of the production system or to quality, and were held in contempt by managers. Shop floors were rife with conflict and tension between first-line managers and assembly-line workers. Charlie Chaplin's portrait of industrial workers in the film *Modern Times* was very close to the mark.

Then something happened: Japanese automobile producers began to eat the Big Three's lunch. They produced vehicles that were higher-quality and cheaper. How was this possible? It turned out that one key to the success of the Japanese automakers was drawing upon the skills and ideas of their production employees, who contributed to quality and efficiency when they were allowed to participate in both production and problem-solving teams and given the power to solve any problems they saw—even the power to stop the assembly line if necessary.[1] It became apparent that this "high-performance work organization" system was superior to the American manufacturing model, and soon a wide range of American industries, both blue- and white-collar, began to adopt it.[2]

The core principles of high-performance systems are investment in training and the human capital of the workforce, broad task design and teamwork, employee involvement in problem-solving, and an atmosphere of cooperation and trust. These principles lead to better performance through several channels: skill, motivation and commitment, and organizational social capital that leads to the sharing of ideas.[3] The human resources literature is now replete with successful examples from blue- and white-collar industries.[4] Low-wage service industries have also been shown to benefit from these systems.[5] And ironically, many hospitals have also adopted these systems.[6]

The analogy should be clear between the organizational principles of high-performance systems—empowering frontline workers—and my arguments in this book regarding the role of direct care workers. Chapter 7 deploys a variety of evidence—examples of home care aides and CNAs playing a more active role; research on other health care occupations that draw on a similar demographic group; and small demonstration programs—to make the case that indeed it is plausible that home care aides could play a broader role than they currently do.

With this evidence in hand, I turn in the following chapters to examining the difficult politics and economics of expanding the role of home care aides. As detailed in chapter 8, these direct care workers are restricted by powerful forces. Happy talk aside, the reality is that they are not respected and are broadly seen as little more than babysitters. Restrictions on their scope of practice prevents them from playing a larger role in the health care system. Financing is another problem: it is very difficult to expand funding and hence to remove the financial caps on the working conditions of home care aides.

Set against these barriers are some reasons for optimism, which I lay out in chapter 9. The basic demographics of the exploding demand for long-term care and the shrinking labor pool able to supply it suggests that pressures will build for reform. In principle, shifts in financing will also help as new models, such as managed care, integrate Medicare and Medicaid. The states should see this logic and take steps to upgrade the role of aides to save on the labor of more expensive occupations. Finally, where they are active, unions are a force pushing for an expanded place for home care aides in the system.

The final chapter pulls together the arguments developed in the book and suggests a way forward.

CHAPTER 7

Direct Care Workers: Opportunities and Evidence

Mount Sinai Hospital, a large teaching hospital in the Mount Sinai Health System in New York, is located at the south edge of East Harlem. The hospital's Visiting Doctors Program sends physicians into the homes of elderly patients, who typically are chronically ill and most of whom also have home care aides. Of the program's 1,300 elderly patients, 80 percent are nursing home–eligible because they have multiple morbidities (several conditions and disabilities).

Care is organized around teams of doctors, nurses, social workers, and home care aides. The nurses and social workers are case managers who coordinate care. Home care aides are trained by the program to help patients manage their health and to communicate with the nurses and doctors as needed. The training provided to the home care aides is "very concrete" and focused on a set of rules, such as, "If you see this, then do that," explained Dr. Theresa Soriano, the founder and former director of the program. Dr. Soriano was very positive about the contribution of the home care aides: "They are amazing people. . . . Their work, the situation they are put in, is not unskilled . . . you [the program] get what you put in." Helena Ross, the lead social worker, added:

> We see the home care aides as very key in helping people to remain in the community, which is one of the goals of our program. We will often go to the home, or set up meetings with the home care aide. We want them to understand the program. . . . We certainly try to include them in any meetings that

have to do with the plan of care, or what the patient's needs are, or [getting] their feedback, all those things. . . . We see the home care aides as crucial people who are there all the time with the patient.

One of the physicians in the Visiting Doctors Program, Jennifer Reckrey, was a young gerontologist who pursued an unusual research interest in the role of home care aides in caring for her patients. She had gone so far as to visit agencies to learn about the training and deployment of home care. I asked her to describe how home care aides work with her and with patients.

There's one particular person who always comes to mind. It was a man in his mid-eighties, who was deaf. . . . He was by himself, except for his aide, Mark, who was there with him eight hours, five days a week. [Mark] basically did everything. First of all, he was the person who communicated on [the patient's] behalf. . . . But [the patient] also had bad leg wounds, and Mark was the one who had been taught by the nurses to wrap them. He did changes in the dressing, but the main thing was the wrapping. He would take exquisite, tender care of the very vulnerable skin and then wrap with gauze to try to help that fluid stay out. He helped heal wounds that had been there for years and years before he started. . . . He was the kind of home care aide who, when the patient was hospitalized and then went to rehab for a period of time, he would go every day to visit him in rehab. . . . Obviously, he wasn't being paid during those times, but he took on the role as a person. . . . The other thing Mark did that was really wonderful, the patient had a lot of anxiety, and most providers in the past had attributed it to his . . . being deaf. . . . Mark would say, "I feel like there's somebody under here who is much more easy to be with, but it's hard for this reason and that reason." He really helped us make the decision that he needed medication for OCD [obsessive-compulsive disorder], and he responded to that extremely well.

I asked Dr. Reckrey whether she could generalize from this example and whether she believed that home care aides could play a larger role. She was emphatic in her reply:

I think mostly. Definitely they can do it. . . . That home care aide can be the bridge to me. . . . I can't think of a single home care aide I've worked with who didn't want to help in some way. They're there, they want to make it better for the person they're caring for.

The goal of this chapter is to provide evidence that, with training, direct care workers—home care aides and certified nursing assistants—can play a broader role and undertake a wider range of responsibilities. Demonstrating this is not easy, however, because there simply have been no rigorously evaluated large-scale demonstrations.

The chapter begins by discussing the functions that direct care workers could serve, drawing from the wider literature on new models of health care delivery. I then present a range of evidence for expanding the role of direct care workers, including rigorous studies of community health care workers (an occupation with a similar demographic profile as home care aides), a number of small studies of efforts to upgrade the role of home care aides, and careful evaluations of nursing home innovations that include a wider role for CNAs. In the final section, I discuss models of training that provide aides with the skills they need to undertake these roles.

NEW MODELS OF HEALTH CARE DELIVERY

If it generally makes sense to draw on the efforts and capacities of the entire health care workforce, what does this mean in practice? And for what kinds of health challenges does this proposition seem relevant? After all, it would not seem sensible to have your brain surgeon be anyone other than a board-certified and experienced practitioner. But this is exactly the problem: the suggestion that home care aides could do a lot more than they are permitted to do evokes the "brain surgeon" reaction, yet the fact is that it is indeed reasonable to expand the scope of practice of home care aides in a great many ways.

Three recent trends in the delivery of health care point directly to an expanded role for home care aides. First is the growing focus on the creation of health care teams, as opposed to the traditional top-down, doctor-focused practices. Second is the increased attention to the management of chronic conditions. The third is new interest in managing transitions from hospitals after acute incidents. The importance of all three trends is supported by research-based evidence, and each creates new opportunities for home care aides to play an expanded role.

Health Care Teams

Just as team production now dominates in manufacturing and many other industries, building effective teams has come to be the mantra in health care reform. In a recent publication, the American Hospital Association argued that "changes are necessary to prepare a workforce able to function in well integrated multi-disciplinary care teams. Perhaps an even greater challenge is the re-education of the current workforce to work in a team-based model of care."[1] The statement explicitly states that nonlicensed personnel—namely, medical assistants and health coaches—should be members of these teams.

In primary care, the diffusion of the patient-centered medical home, which is a team model, is seen as a major objective. This message is reinforced by one of the gurus of the team model of primary care, Dr. Thomas Bodenheimer, who recently wrote that in an ideal practice, "patients with one or two chronic conditions could be cared for by a team whose non-clinician members—under physician supervision—led planned visits, ideally for groups of patients, focused on patient education and lifestyle change, clinical data tracking, and medication."[2] A recent review of cases by the National Health Policy Forum found that the delegation of many medical functions to nonphysician team members resulted in substantial cost savings.[3]

The idea of health care teams speaks not only to the role of aides but also to the need for a deeper reform: the integration of the long-term care team with the medical team.[4] The separation of these two spheres weakens both the quality of medical care and the quality of life for patients.

Management of Chronic Conditions

The management of chronic conditions is a major challenge for the health care system, with respect to both quality of life and costs. The Blue Cross Blue Shield Association reports that more than 133 million people in this country have one or more chronic conditions and two-thirds of older Americans have two or more.[5] The best thinking today points to the central role of health coaches in managing chronic conditions at a reasonable cost. One review characterized their role as follows:

> Health coaching encompasses five principal roles: (1) providing self-management support, (2) bridging the gap between clinician and patient, (3) helping patients navigate the health care system, (4) offering emotional support and (5) serving as a continuity figure. . . . Coaches train patients in seven domains of self-management support: providing information, teaching disease-specific skills, promoting healthy behaviors, imparting problem-solving skills, assisting with the emotional impact of chronic illness, providing regular follow up and encouraging people to be active participants in their care.[6]

An example of a practice that makes considerable use of health coaches is Iora Health, a primary health care practice headquartered in Massachusetts with offices in several states. Health coaches at Iora have a range of educational backgrounds, but a number of them have only a high school degree. Formal training lasts four weeks and is followed by an extended period of supervised on-the-job training. Their day begins with a "huddle" of the entire care team; then the coaches, armed with a task list for each patient, work the phones or, on occasion, visit people in their homes. Their focus is twofold: helping people navigate the health care system and promoting behavior change. Iora avoids scope of practice limitations, which the leadership believes "has to do with people protecting their jobs," and is convinced that "with the right supervision and the right tools," health coaches can play a central role in their delivery system.

Another example of what is possible is found in New York's Union Health Center, where patients are treated by teams that include a doctor, a nurse, and a health coach who is a medical assistant. The demographics of medical assistants are similar to those for home care aides and CNAs, although they do receive more training. When a medical assistant is hired at the center, they spend at least two years in that role as traditionally defined, but they also receive additional training in communications and diabetes management. After those two years, if they wish, they are then trained as a health coach and become more active members of the team. Audrey Lum, the center's chief clinical officer, described the role:

So a provider sees a patient newly diagnosed with diabetes. Starts them on meds, talks to them. "We need to monitor your blood glucose levels and stuff. I want you to see the health coach." It's about establishing relationships. "You're going to establish a relationship with Joann." Joann is the health coach. . . . Initially, she sits with [the patient]. It's about a forty-five-minute visit. They go through things, but she says, "So tell me how you're feeling. There are a lot of things we can work on, but what is the one thing that you think is really affecting you and your diabetes?" "Well, I eat a lot when I'm stressed and I'm stressed at work." So she'll modify, she'll create a plan. The provider knows she has diabetes, but she doesn't know this is what's happening. So the health coach says, "Okay. Let's talk about the plate method. There's this plate method that we have, and it can help you. I can talk to you about snacking." What she does is she creates a plan of care, but she's negotiating with the patient because she's letting the patient pick and choose what they want to work on. So then she says, "We can do these after visits, face to face." She says, "I'm really busy working. I can't do this." "How about if we support each other? I support you by calling you. We can do it over the phone when you're at lunch for ten to fifteen minutes." So they negotiate that. So it's all about this. The relationship that's being built is because the patient knows now that there's more support than her getting sick and coming back to the clinic.

A study tracking patients at Union Health Center over a four-year period showed statistically significant improvements in blood pressure, cholesterol, and blood markers for diabetes.[7] In addition, there were reductions in emergency room costs and other acute care expenditures. The study concluded that utilizing medical assistants as health coaches "created new pathways for people who don't necessarily have advanced educational training. Abilities such as communication proficiency and emotional intelligence are rewarded."[8]

Managing Transitions in Care

The challenge of transitions—the point at which a patient leaves the hospital—was well described in a recent publication by the United Hospital Fund:

Transitions in care for people with chronic illnesses, especially older adults, are frequent, costly, and risky. Nearly one in five Medicare patients admitted to a hospital is readmitted within 30 days of discharge. . . . Many re-hospitalizations are the result of inadequate discharge planning, rushed communications resulting in medication and other errors, and failures to coordinate care with primary care providers or others responsible for the patient after hospital discharge. Even when inadequate hospital discharges do not result in 30-day readmissions, they may be missed opportunities for preventing problems with patient care and readmissions within a few months.[9]

One consequence of poor transitions is that patients end up in expensive nursing homes instead of returning to their own home for care. A recent study found that 75 percent of variation in health care costs across regions is accounted for by differences in after-hospital (post-acute care) treatment.[10] So there is a strong incentive to find cheaper post-acute options.

Addressing this problem has become a central goal of health care reform, and Medicare now penalizes hospitals with excessive readmission rates.[11] The community-based Care Transitions Program—based on demonstration programs funded by the John A. Hartford Foundation and the Robert Wood Johnson Foundation—now provides support for partnerships between hospitals and community-based organizations to improve transition services for Medicare patients. In addition, the United Hospital Fund has developed a model that supports family caregivers and includes them as empowered members of the care team. Family caregivers participate in discharge planning, receive some training in medication management and other relevant clinical issues, and are involved in follow-up check-ins after discharge. An evaluation of this model was positive, and this idea of enhancing the role of family members could easily be extended to home care aides.[12]

A recent review of the research literature and results from randomized demonstrations (the gold standard of medical research) reported enormous potential savings from improved transitional care models and from health coaching.[13] These savings, amounting to over $250 billion a year, come from reducing hospital and emergency room admissions and readmissions and from better managing chronic conditions such as obesity, diabetes, and heart conditions. Two elements of the transitions and coaching models are "regular contact with patients" and "coaching to train patient self-management skills and facilitate behavior change."[14] It seems highly likely that a trained home care aide—a person who is not only in contact with the patient on a daily basis but also in contact with the professional care team—could play an important role in achieving these goals.

Returning to Dr. Reckrey, she described another possible role for home care aides:

> To me, that idea of a patient navigator, who can . . . help people in the system take care of their health more broadly, would be . . . an advocate and a bridge . . . somebody who [has] more knowledge of the health care system than the person they're caring for. . . . [A patient navigator] doesn't have to be a professional, somebody who has gone to medical school or nursing school, but [someone who can] be that bridge that links them to the health care system and keeps them healthy and can deal with whatever that happens to be. For some people, it's monitoring medical things, but for many people it's a somewhat [less]complex role.

EVIDENCE FOR THE EXPANDED ROLE OF HOME CARE AIDES

The foregoing discussion suggests that expanding the scope of home care aides' work would fit in well with current thinking about how to improve health care delivery. But what is the evidence that such expansion would be successful? Thirty years ago, an expert on home care wrote that the relationship between the quality of home care aides' work and their impact on clients was an "untested, though reasonable, assumption."[15] Amazingly, today it still is.

In a field, medicine, that typically conducts serious large-scale evaluations of treatments, there has been virtually no serious large-scale research on the role of home care aides and the possibility of enhancing their role. By contrast, the literature on the training, role, and staffing of nurses and the outcome consequences of different approaches to their job is massive. There is a sparse literature on the role of CNAs, but nothing even approaching this for home care aides, despite the fact that there are roughly as many aides as there are nurses and aides have more "face time" with patients. This neglect reflects, at best, the invisibility of aides in the health care delivery system; at worst, it may derive from the low repute in which they are held.

Faced with this reality, I begin my analysis by piecing together evidence from a range of sources. I examine the impact of community health workers (CHWs), whose work has been assessed to some degree and whose demographic profile is similar to that of home care aides. I describe innovations in the role of CNAs and then report the results of a series of small demonstrations that expanded the role of home care aides. I also report what some medical professionals have to say about the potential impact of the home care aides with whom they have worked. None of this is as satisfying as a full-blown demonstration program, but taken as a whole, this weaving together of evidence does strongly suggest that there is much to be gained by broadening the role of home care aides.

Evidence from a Comparable Occupation

Community health workers are nonlicensed members of the health care team who, as the term implies, work on the ground—in their homes and neighborhoods—on a range of health care issues. Some of their activities, such as helping people sign up for health insurance, are not part of our story. However, in some settings CHWs engage in health coaching, and since the demographics and backgrounds of CHWs tend to be very similar to those of home care aides and CNAs, any evidence of their positive impact is helpful in thinking through what is possible.

As an occupation, community health workers have been around a long time, particularly in developing countries, where they have played a core role in supplementing health care delivery in settings where highly trained personnel are scarce. In these settings, the effectiveness of these lay workers has been widely evaluated, with positive results.[16] In the United States, a substantial growth in interest in CHWs in recent years has been fueled by a remarkably active advocate community. (Indeed, using this movement as a case study of the politics of occupational formation would make for a fascinating project.) There is now enough evidence regarding their effectiveness that it is helpful to consider their work as an analog to what home care aides might do.

One impressive CHW project is City Health Works in Harlem, which works with a clinic at Mount Sinai Hospital and focuses on patients with diabetes. The City Health Works team consists of a care manager (who is either a registered nurse or a licensed nutritionist) and eight community health workers. The program is built around "motivational interviewing," a now widely used approach that comes out of the substance abuse field. The idea is to provide engaging and nonjudgmental interactions that "work on the present." The CHWs visit clients in their homes and, in a very structured program, work with them over the course of thirteen visits on eating, exercise, depression, and a range of other factors in managing their condition and improving the results of their regular blood tests. They do not offer medical advice, but do check for signs of trouble (for example, by looking at patients' feet) and alert the care manager if necessary. The CHWs focus on education and motivation. One of them described her training to me:

> We went to do training for the diabetes and to learn to know . . . the condition, how to treat it. Especially what we do as coaches is to help people to get control of their condition and not to let the condition control their lives. That is done through [not] eating bad and salty food. Also making sure they are going to their appointments, they are taking their medications, and they are doing some physical activity. . . . We were also taught about motivational interviews and how to approach the client that has this condition of diabetes type II. Asking questions and seeing where they were mentally about their condition. . . . They are the ones that are making the decisions. We are just there to guide them.

The impact of City Health Works has not been assessed via random assignment. The organization has collected pre- and post-data on its first 100 clients, however, and these show that 83 percent experienced a reduction in blood indicators for diabetes (HgA1c) and also reductions in their blood pressure readings.

These results are suggestive, but because the intervention is linked to an intensive clinic housed at Mount Sinai, more work is needed to isolate the impact of health coaching per se. A full random assignment evaluation of another CHW program at the University of Pennsylvania does isolate the impact, and the results are strong. In addition, the demographics of the Penn CHWs match very closely those of home care aides.

The Penn Center for Community Health Workers' IMPaCT program, in operation for over five years, uses around twenty-five CHWs to assist patients in their hospital discharge process, in remaining connected to their primary care doctors and specialists, in following instructions regarding diet and medicine and exercise, and in maintaining emotional stability while they deal with their circumstances. The patients are either on Medicaid or uninsured. Two-thirds of the CHWs have only a high school degree; most of the remaining third have a two-year college degree. After four weeks of classroom-based training, they shadow a senior CHW, and then they work on their own under a supervisor (who typically has a master's in social work).

A randomized trial found that patients working with CHWs were more likely to obtain timely post-hospital primary care, to show greater improvements in mental health, to have better communication with their providers, and to be less likely to experience multiple readmissions. There were no differences in measures of physical health or medication adherence.[17]

In addition to these examples, a recent review by the Urban Institute was supportive of the impact of CHWs:

> The strongest evidence is found for improving immunization rates and promoting breast feeding . . . interventions with easily documented outcomes. Some support is also found for effectiveness in improving client knowledge . . . helping clients manage childhood asthma . . . and managing client hypertension. . . . There is a growing, though informal, consensus that CHWs can effect change in the communities they serve.[18]

Evidence from Home Care Aides

After offering some evidence that nonlicensed health workers demographically similar to home care aides can have a positive impact on health outcomes, I now turn to more direct evidence about whether an expanded scope of practice for home care aides is feasible and whether it would lead to better outcomes for clients. As I noted earlier, there is no large demonstration that can nail the issue. Instead, we can only examine a series of smaller examples, none of which is perfect but which taken as a group add up to a plausible conclusion.

Eyes, Ears, and Continuity   At the most basic level, a central role for aides can be summarized by the three words "eyes, ears, continuity." "Eyes and ears" are important because the home care aide is the person who spends the most time with the client and is in the best position to alert other members of the health team when something changes or goes wrong. But of course, in order to play this role home care aides' training and skills need to be upgraded. Continuity (the opposite of the high turnover that characterizes much of the industry) obviously plays a role, not only because having the same aide over time is comforting to the client, but also because continuity increases the aide's knowledge of the client, making her eyes and ears more effective.

It is common sense to expect that high levels of home care aide turnover would lead to worse outcomes for clients because of the loss of continuity of care from someone who knows the client's situation and needs, as well as the loss of companionship. A meta-review of the literature supports the importance of continuity of care from a range of providers, but as is true for virtually everything else that concerns home care aides, there is little solid research testing this idea.[19] (For example, a recent large-scale study of continuity in home health care ignored home care aides and asked only about nurses.)[20] That said, there has been some work on the impact of high turnover of CNAs in nursing homes; this research tends to find a negative impact on quality at high levels of turnover.[21] In a conversation with a doctor who is positive about the potential role of home care aides, we discussed the possibility that she and other doctors would incorporate home care aides into health care transitions and coaching. She pointed to the importance of continuity in terms of making it easier for doctors to work with home care aides:

> It feels a little like the problem has that catch-22. If the home care aide is the same home care aide who has been there forever, you teach them once. It's different than if there's a lot of turnover. . . . If people come in and out of the hospital, they get other people assigned. You go through this all again and what you're teaching, and how that person gets in touch with you.

To get a concrete sense of these points I sat down with some gerontologists to learn what they thought of their clients' home care aides and whether they believed that these aides could contribute to the health care team. Here is a typical reaction:

> Doctor: I always write the name of the caregiver on the chart. I like to know, for medical reasons too, how long they've been with the patient. Because if they're brand-new, they may not know the patient. Or if they're filling in, they may not know the patient. . . . I tell them, "You can always call," and

we get a lot of calls from them. I think that is so important. If either the patient or the family are paying this person to be with the patient, they're the eyes and ears of the patient. They know what's going on with the patient, more than the daughter who has got a full-time job.

Author: Can you give me an example?

Doctor: Right. I think of my "goddess" yesterday. It's an elderly couple. They're both my patients. The daughter lives on the West Coast . . . but the patients have two amazing, paid, round-the-clock caregivers. They change off. They both have dementia, the husband and wife. The husband about a month ago developed pneumonia, wound up in the hospital. The home care aide would come into the hospital because, if you've been in the hospital, people get more delirious and it is very important to have a familiar face with the patient. So the home care aide stayed with him in the hospital. . . . It was one of those situations where, yes, he could have had rehab, but he had such great care at home, twenty-four-hour care, that it was better that he went home. And his wife missed him. So they discharged him after five days. I saw him yesterday, and he was so happy to be home.

The home care aide, Monica, was the only person who knew this patient for years at home, [was] with him in the hospital, was with him in the nursing home, and then says, "Hey, we've got to get him home." He had a lot of medical problems, that's what I was dealing with yesterday. But Monica was the one who brought in all his discharge summary, brought in his pill bottles, told me exactly, "He seems a little short of breath at night." Told me about his urinary problems, told me about his eating. She was the one who was with him throughout all these settings. Which, in the world of ambulance and hospital, none of us do anymore.

Senior Aides Senior home care aides are an innovation of Cooperative Home Care Associates and PHI working with Independence Care Systems, the affiliated insurance company. The senior home care aide is essentially a supervisor who visits other home care aides in the clients' homes and offers advice, support, and some additional on-site training. The senior home care aides receive substantially more training (240 hours) than regular home care aides. The training has two components. The first is listening, observing, and reporting skills. The second is understanding chronic conditions (diabetes, urinary tract infections, cardiac issues, pain) and learning to recognize and respond to these conditions. There is no scope of practice expansion.

In many ways, senior home care aides represent a "back to the future" innovation: in the early 1990s, New York City's Human Resource Administration tested the impact of a "field support home care aide" who performed the same functions as today's senior home care aide. That effort found that turnover of field support home care aides was reduced relative to that of regular home care aides, but funding to continue the program was not forthcoming.[22] The present-day senior home care aide initiative also seems likely to reduce turnover and improve the functioning of regular home care aides, but the lack of a control group limits our ability to be certain about this expectation.

"Grand-aides" receive 180 hours of training beyond basic home health aide certification and are, in the words of the program, "nurse extenders" who have a large patient panel (over 200 patients), visit homes, and report back to the nurse on the clients' condition.[23] For example, they look in medicine cabinets and report the contents to the nurse. If the client has a rash, they take a picture and transmit it to the nurse. Those implementing this model have made no effort to modify nurse practice acts or change the delegation of duties, and so essentially all that grand-aides do is observe and communicate. There is a strong flavor of condescension among the advocates of the model: its original name was the "Grandparent Corp," and the program director said that what he looked for were people who could play the role of "good grandmothers."[24] With pay that averages $25,000 a year, grand-aides are paid only slightly more than the typical home care aide. They play no role in long-term care, and so at best the program demonstrates that home care aides can be trained in other roles.

Dementia Home Care Aides   The New York chapter of the Alzheimer's Association runs a well-regarded program that trains home care aides in managing dementia clients. This is one of the most important skill sets that a home care aide can have, and an aide who has received specialized training and is effective in this role is a valuable asset for clients, their families, and the rest of the medical team. The evidence for the high regard in which the training is held is that other training agencies in the city have replicated (or "borrowed") it.

The training program is conducted one day a week for seven weeks. Home care aides hear about it through the grapevine, and either their agency sends them or they take the initiative to sign up and to pay the $350 fee.

The training consists of exercises aimed at making the experience of Alzheimer's vivid and understandable, simulations that demonstrate how to handle various situations, and a great deal of discussion and support around the home care aide's experiences. After going through a particularly challenging exercise aimed at simulating the effect of Alzheimer's on a patient's perception of the world, a home care aide commented that it "opened my eyes, made me realize how a person with Alzheimer's feels every day of their life. It made me so sympathetic to their struggle." More to the point are the extensive discussions about how to handle common situations and the supportive discussions in which home care aides describe their experiences and get feedback from the instructor and colleagues.

Unfortunately, no formal evaluation of the impact of this training is available. That said, my conversations with home care aides made it clear that their commitment to working with these clients deepened as a result of the training and that they perceived their skills as having improved substantially. I interviewed a woman whose parent's home care aide had received the training, and she could not stop talking about how much it meant and the degree to which the training improved the quality of the interaction between her parent and the aide.

Modest but Hopeful Evaluations

As I have noted, what sociologists term an "unobtrusive indicator" of the low repute in which home care aides are held is the lack of large-scale evaluations of how their roles and their impact might be expanded. One recent study did examine whether innovations in technology could improve communication between aides and medical personnel, but beyond this the few demonstrations that exist are small and the evaluations, while serious, are typically not quite up to the standards that an academic journal would require.[25] But these efforts nonetheless add to our accumulating evidence that home care aides can do more and that clients benefit when they do. The point is to show that an enlarged role is possible and that most home care aides respond to the opportunity. Truth in advertising requires that we also acknowledge that an enlarged role for home care aides does not translate into better wages or benefits.

How to move from an expanded scope of practice to improved working conditions is the topic of another chapter. Here I am concerned with what might be termed an existence proof: that there is indeed evidence that it is possible to expand the job.

The Visiting Nurse Service of New York (VNSNY), the largest home health agency in the United States, has a history of interest in experimenting with the role of home care aides. Carol Raphael, the longtime CEO, recounted the organization's attempts to expand the role of home care aides. The "nurses went bonkers," "the union insisted on a new job classification," and "managers resisted because it was too much trouble." Nonetheless, the organization did manage to mount two modest demonstrations.

In one of these demonstrations, the idea was to train home care aides as health coaches to work with cardiac patients upon discharge. The manager of this program noted with some irony that even though their foundation funding enabled them to offer it to hospitals at no cost, it took six months to find a hospital willing to try it. No one believed in home care aides. "They don't understand the capability of this workforce. They think they are only able to cook, clean, and bath people."

Eventually, New York University Hospital agreed to the demonstration. For thirty days after discharge, the home care aides met with patients to go over their care plan, to encourage them to stick with their exercise program, and to engage in motivational interviewing (as described earlier in the section on health coaching at City Health Works). The program was designed for one hundred patients, but for a variety of reasons only thirty-three were enrolled. These thirty-three patients were subsequently compared to a control group. Readmission rates of the control and treatment groups did not differ; however, the patients who completed the health coaching program "reported significant improvements in self-care maintenance and management of heart failure symptoms and preliminary evidence suggests that the program may improve patients' performance of health maintenance behaviors, such as diet and exercise, and ability to manage symptoms effectively." In addition, in the words of the evaluation team,

the Health Coaches we interviewed felt that their transition from Home Health Aide to Health Coach was relatively seamless and expressed a sense of enjoyment with their new work, especially when compared with their prior role as a Home Health Aide. One Health Coach stated that she felt less like a "housekeeper" and more like a "partner" in patient care.[26]

I asked the manager whether, in light of the success of this demonstration, she believed that insurance companies would pay for it and hospitals would incorporate it into their care plans. She thought not. The hospital administrators with whom she had talked wanted to use registered nurses instead of home care aides, and the insurance companies were just not interested.

In the second demonstration, home care aides assisted patients with physical therapy. The aides received four days of training in providing care to orthopedic patients and working as a team member with the assigned physical therapist. The home care aides participated in team meetings and were given cell phones to communicate with the therapists and VNSNY staff. Compared to a control group, the clients showed statistically significant improvement in the number of ADL deficiencies for which they needed assistance. According to the evaluation team:

> Perhaps one of the more substantial changes we observed during the evaluation period concerned the level of collaboration between [aides] and professional rehabilitation staff. When [aides] were first surveyed, they rated their level of collaboration with professional therapists significantly lower than aides in the control group (2.9 out of 4 among [aides] compared to 3.5 out of 4 among controls). However, the [aides'] average rating for the six survey questions concerning collaboration increased significantly between the start and end of the evaluation period. This finding suggests that the various program initiatives were successful in encouraging professional rehabilitation staff and [aides] to work more closely together. . . . We did find . . . that patients in the intervention group were significantly more likely to report that their [aide] guided them through each exercise and made sure they were transferring and performing exercises properly.[27]

Two demonstrations in California also point in a positive direction. One small effort, the Enhanced Home Care Pilot Program, was conducted in 2012 at the St. John's Well Child and Family Center.[28] In this program, ninety-seven pairs of home care aides and clients were randomly selected and the aides were trained in medication management, mental health, nutrition, and physical skills such as lifting. In addition, the home care aides were encouraged to communicate with health care providers through the care coordinator, a new position created as part of the demonstration. Assessments showed that medication noncompliance rates decreased, there were fewer ER and hospital visits, the number of unhealthy days decreased, and 85 percent of the clients strongly agreed that their health had benefited from the intervention.

A second demonstration was much larger, but as is true in much of the field, the evaluation suffered from flaws stemming from the disorganized long-term care system. A large federal grant supported sixty hours of classroom training and thirteen hours of on-site training for over six thousand consumer-directed aides who would otherwise have received no instruction. In addition, an effort was made to integrate aides more deeply in health care teams. Consumer-and-aide pairs opted into the demonstration (hence there was no random assignment) and were drawn from six health plans. Before-and-after data were collected on emergency room visits and number of in-patient days spent in a hospital.

An irony, of course, was that the amount of training offered was an increase from the baseline of zero for consumer-directed aides, but remained below the minimum requirement for agencies in New York. This ambitious effort ran into two big problems. The fact that it proved difficult to convince professionals on the care teams to take the time to participate in the integration training reinforces my point about the general disrespect toward home care aides. Additionally, the quality of the evaluation data varied considerably across the six health insurance plans. Nonetheless, the results were suggestive: in the one plan that provided good data, the sample size was small but did point to a nontrivial post-training reduction in emergency room visits and in-patient days.[29]

Summary

What does all this add up to? Each of the studies cited here had significant weaknesses that, truth be told, would preclude publication in a quality peer-reviewed journal. In some there was no random assignment. Where there was random assignment, the treatment was not consistent across sites, making it hard to know just what was being tested. In other evaluations, there were multiple interventions (for example, training and selection) in the same demonstration, and so it is hard to discern just what was the driver of impact. Finally, most of the demonstrations were simply too small to give us a strong level of confidence.

All of these weaknesses reflect the fundamental nature of the field—it is just not taken seriously by large funders and governments. That said, the question remains: when these studies are considered as a whole, and when we add to them the evidence from related fields with similar demographics, are we convinced that home care aides can have a real impact on outcomes if their scope of practice could be broadened and they were appropriately deployed and trained? I think it is reasonable to answer yes to this question.

I now turn to certified nursing assistants. The discussion that follows speaks directly to the role they could play, but it also reflects back on the potential of home care aides, given the substantial similarity in the demographics and education of the two groups.

CERTIFIED NURSING ASSISTANTS

As I have already noted, even though nursing homes will continue to be an important source of long-term services and supports, they are far from popular, among both their residents and the low-wage CNAs who staff them. In the face of widespread concerns about inadequate and often dangerous conditions, regulatory authorities have tightened standards and monitoring and developed a rating system accessible to potential residents and their families. But of equal importance—and of greater interest to our focus on low-wage direct care workers—the national "culture change" movement seeks to reconsider the organization and operation of nursing homes to improve quality and make them more patient-centered. At the core of this effort has been a reconsideration of the role of CNAs.

In culture change nursing homes, CNAs are seen as more integrated members of the health care team, and in some versions of culture change their role is enlarged in very substantial ways. This change is important to the themes of this book for two reasons. First, since there will always be some people who need a nursing home level of care, this enhancement of the role of CNAs is important because it points to ways to improve the experience of residents. Second, to the extent that an enlarged scope of practice for CNAs in culture change nursing homes leads to better outcomes, this supports my argument that direct care workers can indeed do more than they are currently permitted to do and that the long-term care system will benefit.

Under the umbrella of the Pioneer Network, some nursing homes now serve as a forum for facilitating these efforts. Examples include the Eden Alternative, Wellspring, and the Green House (GH) model. Each of these is a distinct implementation (with, as we shall see, Green House adding innovations in physical space), but the broad idea is to maximize resident autonomy. Surveys of culture change facilities find that direct care workers undertake a wider range of tasks than comparable workers in traditional facilities.[30] Christine Bishop, in her review of these models, analogizes them to high-performance work systems in manufacturing, which expand the role of frontline workers.[31]

Probably the most elaborate and extensive rethinking and enlarging of the role of CNAs can be found in the Green House model. The Green House project began in 2003 in Tupelo, Mississippi; by 2015, 174 Green House facilities were serving almost 1,800 residents nation-wide. The model has a number of distinct aspects, such as small home living arrangements, private rooms, residents' control over their time, and flexible eating schedules. For our purposes, the key point is that the CNAs, who are called "Shabbaz," work in self-managed teams and have considerably broadened roles in carrying out their tasks, from cooking, housekeeping, and implementing care plans to working with residents on their daily activities. As one comparison of a sample of Green House facilities with traditional facilities noted, "In the GH homes, caregivers were responsible for an average of seven non-interactive tasks (for example, cleaning, cooking meals) and nine interactive tasks (for example, participating in activities, taking blood pressures), all of which were more prevalent in GH than in legacy homes."[32]

I visited a Green House nursing home, the Leonard Florence Center for Living in Chelsea, Massachusetts. Having spent time in a considerable number of nursing homes, I noticed right away that this one was different. The atmosphere was homelike, and the residents were not stockpiled in hallways but rather moving about the facility—on their own, with walkers, with wheelchairs—or else sitting and chatting. Each pod had a kitchen and a living room.

Perhaps the most remarkable feature of this particular facility—one that is not a part of the Green House model but speaks to the commitment of Barry and Adam Berman, who run the facility—is the ALS unit. Largely designed by Steve Saling, an ALS patient and former architect, the entire Green House facility can be controlled by ALS patients via their eye movements, which are transmitted to a networked computer on their wheelchairs. Doors open, elevators respond, the HVAC system is controlled, and even the televisions in residents' rooms respond to eye movements.[33] The system uses off-the-shelf components, and as Saling himself said (through his computer, also controlled by eye movements), "The twenty-first century has arrived for the disabled," adding, "my cup was cut in half but it is now full."

The Green House model is important to the argument developed here because it shows that the role of CNAs can be expanded. Whether this particular model is the answer to improving nursing homes generally is a different question. The capital costs are extensive (Leonard Florence cost $23 million to build), and it would be very expensive to retrofit existing facilities. In fact, the larger organization that Leonard Florence is part of is retrofitting another facility to be what might be termed "Green House Lite." Forty resident floors will be broken up into two twenty-resident units with kitchens and living areas. But the rooms will remain semiprivate, and it is unclear whether the staffing of CNAs will increase to Green House levels. The retrofit is costing $15 million, well beyond what Medicaid reimbursement rates support. Only being part of a larger nonprofit with a substantial endowment and donor base makes it possible for these facilities to upgrade in this way.

Efforts to upgrade the role of CNAs are not limited to Green House models or even entirely to culture change nursing homes. I visited another nursing home, NewBridge in Dedham, Massachusetts (a subsidiary of Hebrew Senior Life), which has created a senior CNA position (they use the terms "resident assistant" and "senior resident assistant"). The CNAs receive an additional 120 hours of training over six months and then perform a range of roles. They mentor other CNAs, helping them with skills such as techniques for safe lifting. Trained in what to look for with respect to a range of changes in health status, they observe patients and report any developments to nurses. They "huddle" with the care team to help with care planning. They interact with the patients' families and often interpret the patient's status for them. They organize activities, such as art shows and music events, that enrich the patients' lives. All of this increased training and the broader range of tasks for low-wage health care workers can pay off for patients in a variety of ways.

Does expansion of the CNA role improve outcomes for residents? Alternatively, do residents suffer because they are getting more attention from less-qualified people? There have been many evaluations of culture change nursing homes in general, and a recent ambitious undertaking is aimed at assessing the impact of the Green House model in particular.

With respect to culture change in general, a recent review of an extensive evaluation literature concluded that there is no evidence of negative effects and strong hints of positive outcomes for residents.[34] A high-quality evaluation utilizing a pre- and post-analysis of culture change facilities and a comparison sample found that, relative to the controls, the culture change sites reduced health-related survey deficiencies (of the sort used by regulators in their checklist) but showed no improvement in the health outcomes of their residents. The authors expected, however, to see these improvements emerge over time.[35]

With respect to the Green House model itself, an early evaluation found much higher levels of resident and family satisfaction.[36] More recently, an extensive evaluation project, supported by the Robert Wood Johnson Foundation, collected data between 2011 and 2014 from twenty-eight Green House homes and fifteen comparison homes and reviewed older data from a large set of Green House and comparison facilities.[37] The authors are cautious about drawing broad conclusions, but do find that hospital readmissions fell in Green House homes and several direct measures of health status improved. Medicare expenditures were reduced. There was also evidence of reduced CNA turnover. With respect to the staff, the researchers concluded that the research

> establishes the importance of communication and collaboration between and among direct care staff and medical care providers to effect good quality care. . . . In GH homes, consistent assignment of universal worker direct care staff, and small homes built around a central living area, allow familiarity with residents and provide opportunities for frequent interactions among staff. If used in an opportune manner, increased multidisciplinary collaboration might lead to early identification and intervention in response to resident change of medical condition, a vital step in quality care.

The bottom line is that a range of innovations in nursing homes do demonstrate that direct care workers can in fact play a more extensive role as part of a care team and have a positive impact on outcomes. In closing this discussion, it seems important to note one major irony. Quite a bit of careful and creative thinking has obviously gone into improving the quality of nursing homes. Additional serious effort has been devoted to evaluation and assessment of innovations. And one part of all this has been rethinking and reassessing the role of CNAs. This is all obviously good and deserves to be applauded. But the sad fact is that no comparable efforts have been made with respect to home care and the role of home care aides, despite the fact that millions more people receive help at home than in nursing homes. But this observation aside, the lesson of culture change innovations as well as other initiatives is that there is considerable scope for upgrading the role of CNAs.

TRAINING

Two questions follow from the foregoing: Are home care aides interested in the broader role that I describe? And can they be successfully trained to undertake these roles?

It would be unrealistic to think that everyone wants to take on new responsibilities. Some of the home care aides whom I interviewed expressed a great deal of satisfaction with the job and were either puzzled or not interested when I raised the issue of, for example, working with clients on healthy lifestyles. Some were simply beyond the point where they could comfortably learn new skills. But many home care aides were eager to take on more responsibility. I observed training sessions at Cooperative Home Care Associates, the Visiting Nurse Service of New York, and the Alzheimer's Association, and in each case I saw home care aides who were focused and involved in learning and who clearly expressed an interest in learning more. I am not in a position to estimate the fraction of all home care aides who are open to additional training and new roles. Certainly the numbers are large, however, and if given the opportunity, many would like to see the fundamental nature of the occupation transformed.

Do we have examples of best practice training that can be successful? What is the evidence that these skills can be imparted and learned? A six-state federal demonstration—the Personal and Home Care Aide State Training

(PHCAST) program, launched in 2010—was intended to identify best training practice, but as I explain later, it was deeply flawed in its design. That said, several smaller state demonstration programs have shown that training can be successful. The California demonstration I described earlier measured the pre- and post-knowledge of aides and showed increases in consumer satisfaction, and a large training program in Washington State also demonstrated that skills can be successfully taught.

When it comes to training home care aides, the best practice organization is certainly PHI, an organization that is very active in public policy issues regarding low-wage health care workers. Its research is widely used; for example, the Congressional Commission on Long-Term Care recently drew on PHI data, as did the U.S. Department of Labor in publishing its economic justification for the changes in minimum wage and overtime coverage rules. But PHI's deepest roots lie in its expertise in training. The PHI curriculum and training philosophy have been widely adopted: for example, three of the six states involved in the PHCAST home care aide training demonstration utilize PHI material, as do many of the Pioneer Network nursing homes that represent best practice in deploying CNAs in nursing homes.

As is far too often the case in the long-term care field, there are very few viable evaluations of training for home care aides. One credible evaluation examined a large training intervention based on the PHI approach. At the core of the PHI model are four components: (1) more hours of training (120 instead of 75); (2) adult-centered learning that focuses less on "chalk and talk" and more on interactive material; (3) training that takes place in the agency (not in clients' homes) and hence provides somewhat more realistic exposure to the realities of the job than school-based programs; and (4) learning in small teams of trainees, peer instructors, and instructors.

This demonstration, which involved well over 1,000 home care aides in three agencies, was combined with a more rigorous selection process in which prospective home care aides were given a realistic view of the work and the agencies had more opportunity to assess the aide applicants prior to the training. This step makes it hard to distinguish the impact of the training from the impact of better selection on subsequent outcomes. However, each of the agencies implemented the selection process somewhat differently while showing more fidelity to the training system, and so it is reasonable to think that improved training played a big role in the positive outcomes.

And what were those positive outcomes? As unfortunately is always the case for long-term care, there are no data on client outcomes. However, the home care aide turnover rate in the demonstration was substantially lower than that of home care aides who were hired at the same time but were not part of the demonstration. The demonstration home care aides expressed broad and enthusiastic satisfaction with the training, with over 75 percent reporting that the training was excellent and 100 percent reporting satisfaction. And to my point, the evidence is clear that the home care aides were interested in the additional material and made the effort to absorb it. I spoke with the head of one of the agencies involved in this demonstration, and she was effusive. She observed that the home care aides loved the training because it was geared to listening to them. Indeed, "everyone found the program so much better," she said, that "we couldn't go back [to the agency's previous practice]."

CONCLUSION

This chapter has provided what might be termed an "existence proof." The aim was to produce a collage of evidence to make the point that home care aides, the very people who are ignored by most of the field and who evoke worries that they might put the cat's eyedrops in their client's eyes, can in fact play a more important role in delivering quality long-term care than they are currently allowed to do. The evidence on this point falls short of the gold standard in medical research, but the fault lies not with home care aides but rather with those who run the system and finance demonstration projects. Perhaps this accumulation of evidence will be convincing that much more is possible than is currently envisioned, much less permitted.

It is also important to be realistic. Claiming that too much is possible does no one any good and can undermine the case for what is truly possible. Several qualifications on this score are important to recognize.

- "Selling" the new role to clients may sometimes be a challenge. In a demonstration in New York run by Cooperative Home Care Associations, PHI, and Independence Care Systems, a surprisingly high number of clients rejected the use of iPads by the home care aide (who was supposed to record the client's conditions) on the grounds that they were being "spied on." An insurance company with which I raised the idea of expanding the role of home care aides thought that some clients might not want their "girls" to do anything other than provide companionship and do housework.

- Not all clients need a home care aide who can do more than is currently allowed. For example, a client who is cognitively capable and simply needs help with some physical tasks (for example, getting dressed) may not need much in the way of health coaching.

- Given this variation in need, acceptance, and capacity, the proposal to expand the role of home care aides can create significant logistical problems for providers. If a more highly trained home care aide works four hours for a client who needs those skills and four hours for a client who does not, how is that home care aide compensated? If the agency wishes to avoid this issue, then scheduling becomes a far more challenging proposition.

- Finally, we may bump up against the realities of consumer-directed care. As we have seen, some consumer-directed states, Washington being the prime example, have made substantial efforts to expand the training and capacity of home care aides. In other states, however, such as California and Massachusetts, any effort to require training is strongly opposed. In these states, where about 70 percent of home care aides are family or friends—many of whom will leave the career when their client dies or no longer needs help—it is not entirely clear what the rationale is for training beyond the basics of safety.

These are all legitimate questions. I raise them now to assure readers that I am not engaged in a pie-in-the-sky exercise. There are certainly management solutions to all of them. Before reaching that point, however, we first have to address the prior question: is any of this even possible given the political and institutional forces that shape our system of long-term care?

CHAPTER 8

Obstacles to Change

I totally believe the home care aides make the difference for patients, and they have not had the opportunity to show it.

These are minimum-wage people.

The first comment is from an interview I conducted with a senior manager at one of the largest home health agencies on the East Coast. She had innovated by initiating several small demonstrations within her agency to expand the role of home care aides, but while the results were promising, the ideas never took hold. She could not get other managers to show interest, and she could not convince payers to raise reimbursement rates in return for an enlarged scope of practice. What is the problem? I asked her. This was her response: lack of opportunity for home care aides to demonstrate their importance.

The second comment was made by the CEO of a large managed care organization. Factually, he was correct: the wages that home care aides receive are low. But this was not his point. In response to a question about scope of practice, he was commenting on the capacity of home care aides to do more than allowed. Over the course of our conversation, it was clear that he was a very decent person and that his managed care organization was quite innovative in the services it provided to clients. But when it came to home care aides, he simply could not see beyond the stereotypes.

I also interviewed two senior managed care managers who were offering a private-pay product to assist families of clients who were leaving the hospital after an acute incident and who wanted a smooth transition to home rather than a nursing facility. The services offered included a care manager who developed a plan and nurses and social workers who executed it. I asked if home care aides could play a role, and the managers (who had both previously worked in a home care agency) were in agreement that this would make sense and save money, but that "it didn't fit their business model." When I asked why, they said that clients would never accept a "girl" playing any substantive role in the process.

This stereotype informed thinking at the federal policymaking level as well. In the course of this research, I interviewed senior federal health care officials, from the top leadership at the Centers for Medicare and Medicaid Services to policy staff in the U.S. Department of Health and Human Services and health care staff in the White House Office of Management and Budget. Everyone expressed sympathy for the economic circumstances of home care aides, but subsequent discussion was discouraging. The HHS policy staff argued that while home care aides could be good companions, there was no reason to think that they could contribute to any positive medical outcomes. At CMS and OMB, the top leadership was deeply familiar with numerous aspects of health care financing and delivery, but much vaguer about long-term care. Other than long-term care insurance, they had little to say (so much so that one senior official did not know that the California model was consumer-directed), and of course, this failure to engage extended to any insight into the circumstances of home care aides or their possible role in the system.

The difficulties in enacting change and the inattention of federal health officials are examples of a theme I keep returning to: that home care aides are not respected and they are not seen as potential partners in a health care team. This frame of thinking is a fundamental challenge, but one that perhaps can be overcome with the kind of evidence presented in chapter 7. But the challenges of change go deeper. This way of thinking is not just a cultural frame but one grounded in politics and economics as well. These challenges represent clashes of interest that can slow reform. Understanding these difficulties is the theme of this chapter.

The political challenges are considerable. There are significant tensions between efforts to expand the scope of practice of home care aides and the perspectives of other health care occupations, notably nurses. Complicating the scope of practice limits is the web of governmental regulations, as well as funding silos, that shape the delivery of long-term care. These regulatory and funding challenges can make reform difficult even if there is general agreement about desirable outcomes.

Second, the advocates themselves are not always on the same page. Important voices in the disability community resist efforts to establish extended training programs for home care aides, and as I discuss later in the chapter, they fought efforts to interpret the Fair Labor Standards Act in a way that provides home care aides with minimum wage and overtime protections. Their opposition stemmed not from any lack of generosity but rather from the quite different implications for sound regulatory policy in the "two worlds" of agency and consumer-directed care. Adding to the tension within the long-term care community, the interests of nursing homes, a powerful lobby, are not the same as the interests of those in favor of home and community-based care.

Finally, the financing system is an obstacle for several distinct reasons. First, and most obvious, is the difficulty of increasing expenditures, which keeps a cap on the compensation and training of home care aides. In addition, the incentive structure is dysfunctional: because long-term care is financed by Medicaid and acute care, for many people, is financed by Medicare, the Medicaid system has little incentive to seek ways to reduce the costs of acute medical care. Put differently, an innovation that permits home care aides to improve medical outcomes would not redound to the benefit of Medicaid per se.

This chapter will work through these challenges, and the next chapter will take up reasons to be optimistic.

THE FUNDING SYSTEM:
AN OBSTACLE TO REFORM

Medicaid is an incredibly complicated program: it serves a range of needs (from children's health to long-term care and everything in between), the federal rules are obtuse (this is an understatement), and being a federal-state program, it is administered in vastly different ways by each state. Here I will keep our focus narrow and examine Medicaid only with respect to long-term care.

Not only is Medicaid the major payer for people who need help, but if we switch our angle of view and ask how important long-term care is for the Medicaid program, we see that it is a very big deal. Overall the elderly and disabled accounted for 24 percent of Medicaid enrollees in 2011 but 63 percent of costs.[1] Long-term services and supports alone accounted for 34 percent of all Medicaid expenditures in 2012.[2]

Even the long-term care components of Medicaid are difficult to understand. There are myriad subprograms, each with somewhat different eligibility standards and each varying across states. The subprograms typically are created via so-called waivers, which enable deviations from the Medicaid legislation. The issuance of these waivers is widely accepted as the way in which the system evolves, but the legacy is a piling up of subprogram on top of subprogram. A large elder law legal bar has grown to help people navigate this system and find ways to receive Medicaid support. But this client perspective is not our focus, and we will touch on it only as necessary. Rather, the goal here is to understand the flow of support that underwrites the provision of services and the employment of home care.

Six characteristics of Medicaid are important to our story: (1) Medicaid is fundamentally a welfare program; (2) the pressure that Medicaid places on state budgets results in a desire to limit expenditures; (3) the considerable variation in policies across states makes it difficult to develop a coherent national response to the challenges; (4) incentives are misaligned; (5) Medicaid's priorities are trending away from institutional (nursing home) care and toward home and community-based care; and (6) the movement today is away from fee-for-service and toward managed care. The first four characteristics are unfortunate and make it difficult to develop a strategy for reconsidering the delivery of long-term care, while the last two offer opportunities as well as risks (which I take up in the next chapter).

The first point to grasp above and beyond anything else is that Medicaid is a welfare program. As such, it carries all the stigma and limitations and political weakness of welfare in America. Social scientists throw around derisive comments such as "this is a welfare program" with perhaps too much abandon, so let us turn to a description of Medicaid from the leading health law textbook:

Though the original goal of Medicaid was to provide mainstream medical care for the poor, payment rates for professionals and providers have been held to such low levels for so many years in most states that Medicaid recipients in most States now receive their health care through a distinctive system of 'welfare medicine.' Eligibility for Medicaid is means tested and recipients are subjected to all the stigma that in our society attaches to being a welfare recipient. . . . The Medicaid program is one of the largest items in the budgets of most states and is always politically controversial and vulnerable.[3]

Medicaid is means-tested, funding is shared by the federal government and the states, the program is administered by the states, and each state has broad (albeit not unlimited) discretion regarding eligibility, generosity, and other program elements. States can also control their caseload through bureaucratic strategies such as making the application process slow and difficult and permitting waitlists for some components of home and community care. All of this variation and local control is characteristic of welfare and not of politically strong popular entitlements such as Social Security and Medicare.

Medicaid Funding

As a practical matter, the core implication of the welfare nature of Medicaid is that its reimbursement rates for services are well below those of Medicare. On average, nationally Medicaid pays providers about 66 percent of what Medicare pays, and this percentage is even lower in a number of states.[4] It is important to understand that there is nothing inherent in Medicaid that requires low reimbursements. The problem is that, in addition to the welfare stigma, considerable funding comes out of state budgets, and this creates competition for funds. Not surprisingly, programs for "poor people" get the short end of the stick. This is true even though many middle-class people end up using Medicaid to finance their long-term care (see appendix E).

The impact of low reimbursement rates was brought home vividly to me when I visited a large East Coast hospital. This institution, one of the nation's health care jewels and admirable in many respects, has two primary care clinics. The clinic for private insurance and private-pay patients is just what one would expect: attractive facilities and access to the best doctors available. But the doctors at this clinic do not accept Medicaid. Patients on Medicaid go to the other clinic, where they are seen by medical students (residents) who are supervised by a few primary care doctors. The clinic is crowded and unattractive. Even though the residents are undoubtedly capable, a patient who returns rarely sees the same person again, and so there is no doctor-patient relationship and no continuity of care.

To get a more vivid sense of the funding process I spoke with a state Medicaid director about how reimbursement rates are set. In an ideal (and naive) view of the world, the rates would be set by asking what is necessary to obtain quality care and what is necessary to compensate providers (doctors, nurses, home care aides) at a decent rate. This is one model. Another would be "last year's rate plus or minus X percent," and a third choice would be a pure log-rolling negotiation with the governor and the administration. Not surprisingly, the Medicaid director answered with a combination of the second and third models. Providers submit costs and requests, but "realpolitik" is what sets the rates.

State Budgets

If the welfare nature of Medicaid is one limitation, another is the funding mechanism. Medicaid is funded by both state and federal appropriations, with the federal share varying inversely with the ratio of the state's per capita income to national per capita income. This formula brings a redistributional element to the program, although states have discretion to undermine it through strict eligibility and benefit policies. However, the real trap of the funding mechanism is that Medicaid has become a huge burden on state budgets. Nationally in 2012, Medicaid spending accounted for a bit over 16 percent of the revenue generated by states from their own sources (taxes and fees on local citizens and businesses), and in some states the burden is considerably higher—for example, 26 percent in New York and 20 percent in Pennsylvania.[5] As a consequence, any call to improve benefit levels or reimbursements (which directly affect the compensation of home care aides) runs up against competing and worthy uses of state funds, education being the prime example. In total in 2012, states spent $181 billion of their own funds on Medicaid, compared to $270 billion on education.[6]

This budgetary trap limits efforts to use Medicaid to improve and expand the provision of long-term care or to improve reimbursement rates for the services provided. In addition, because Medicaid gives states substantial discretion in setting reimbursement rates, the temptation to squeeze them is irresistible.

Reimbursements, Margins, and Wages

The welfare character of Medicaid and the pressure on state budgets come together to sharply limit reimbursements to providers. As a direct consequence of low reimbursement rates, agencies that employ home care aides are limited in the compensation they can offer. The broader consequence is that there is very little money in the system to enable experimentation with new modes of care provision. Medicaid is an iron cage that, as currently structured, limits what is possible.

Agencies that rely on Medicaid were quite profitable in the past but now seem to be under considerable financial pressure, and their margins appear to be shrinking. The rating agency Standard & Poor's reports that,

> owing to both federal and state budget deficits, the federal government and most (if not all) states constantly consider ways to reduce the level of Medicaid funding—for example, by cutting payments to providers—while still maintaining the list of Medicaid benefits that are covered. Therefore, Medicaid revenues for those participating in the program are likely to fall in coming years.[7]

Although not a big part of the overall system, Medicare-focused agencies (often termed "certified agencies") are more profitable than Medicaid agencies. The more than 12,000 Medicare-certified agencies, like nursing homes, are more focused on lucrative nursing and physical therapy services; as a result, their financial margins are comfortable, a bit over 12 percent.[8]

Margins in the private-pay world—particularly among the chains entering the business—also appear to be comfortable, mainly because they avoid Medicaid and rely on clients who can afford large fees. In many cases, however, these agencies pay the same low wages to home care aides as do Medicaid agencies. Candace Howe, who has carefully studied the industry, offers data suggesting that the cost of entry is very low and the margins substantial.[9]

Consistent with this was the information shared with me on hourly pay rates for home care aides and the revenue they receive for these services in my interviews with a large chain operating in twenty-two states. For example, in New Jersey (a relatively high-wage state), home care aides were paid at an hourly rate of $9.50 (with no benefits) while clients were billed at $16.50 per hour. Even taking administrative costs into account, this is a good business. The profitability of the private-pay agency world is reinforced by an industry report that the median margin of the agencies under review (80 percent of which were private-pay or long-term insurance agencies) is 21.9 percent.[10]

That there is money to be made by paying low wages and charging high fees was further ratified by an investment adviser who commented in a financial publication that

> investors are pursuing deals in personal care services, which includes skilled home health care, hospice, and unskilled home care. One theme that we are seeing emerge is investors pursuing personal care services companies that use home health aides to enable individuals to stay in their homes versus institutional settings. Companies . . . are attractive because they provide the opportunity to monitor individuals with the absolute lowest cost employee, an unskilled home health aide, and potentially avert more acute, costly and dangerous episodes for the patient. These aides are minimum-wage type workers.[11]

Variation Across States

The remarkable variation across states is illustrated by data in table 8.1, which shows the variation in per resident expenditures for long-term care across states, from a high of $1,169 to a low of $167. This variation is explained by neither the wealth of the state nor the size of the universe of need, and it is certainly not what we would expect in a well-designed system. Variation across states is common on many other dimensions. In a recent survey of states, the Kaiser Family Foundation reports considerable dispersion with respect to the income levels required for eligibility (which can be as low as 100 percent of the federal poverty line [FPL]), the functional requirements (how disabled a person needs to be in order to be eligible), and the prevalence of waitlists.[12]

All of this variation points to the truth of a common refrain regarding Medicaid: "If you understand one state, then you understand one state." This variation, along with the built-in pressure on state budgets, is what makes it

Table 8.1   Medicaid Expenditures for Long-Term Care: The Six Most
Generous States and the Six Least Generous States, 2015

States	Total LTSS Expenditures per Resident	Percentage of LTSS Directed to Home and Community Care for Older People and People with Physical Disabilities	Percentage of LTSS Directed to Home and Community Care for People with Developmental Disabilities
States with highest expenditures per resident			
New York	$1,169.69	48.1%	68.7%
Connecticut	873.55	27.8	73.7
Rhode Island	782.75	21.8	95.4
West Virginia	740.48	30.1	83.2
Alaska	724.69	63.4	97.9
Minnesota	721.09	66.8	86.2
National average	464.35	40.2	72.3
States with lowest expenditures per resident			
Florida	262.24	24.0	70.9
Georgia	260.77	25.5	91.4
Arizona	237.13	44.4	96.4
Nevada	176.92	34.9	79.4
New Mexico	175.71	n/a	91.9
Utah	167.25	23.0	73.1

Source: Eiken et al. 2015, tables Y, AQ, and AP.
Note: LTSS = long-term services and supports.

very hard to think in an integrated way about how to move forward on efforts to reform the financing of long-term care.

Misaligned Incentives

An additional problem with how long-term care is financed is that the incentive structure is wrong. Medical care (what is termed "acute care") is typically provided by Medicare while long-term care is provided by Medicaid, and therefore the Medicaid long-term care world has no incentive to reduce medical expenditures. Innovations to this end are not in the narrow interest of the system and so are frequently not pursued. This is why—to pick a canonical example—agencies simply instruct home care aides to call 911 if there is a problem, rather than train them in how to prevent the problem in the first place. This problem has long been understood; two decades ago, in the mid-1990s, Robyn Stone argued for the integration of long-term care and acute care in a unified financing system.[13] In the next chapter, I discuss so-called dual demonstrations that attempt to address this issue.

THE DIFFICULTY OF EVEN SMALL CHANGES

Turning to challenges beyond finance, I focus first on conflicts around occupational boundaries.

The health care field is rife with rivalries between occupations as they struggle for dominion over a particular set of diseases, treatments, or services. This culture of competition goes back to the days when physicians fought it out with faith healers for the basic right to treat illness.[14] Today the controversies continue. For example, optometrists who wish to perform Lasik eye surgery or treat glaucoma find themselves engaging with ophthalmologists who insist on keeping these procedures under their own purview and argue that patients will be at risk otherwise.[15] My point is not to argue the merits of either case, but rather to highlight the occupational competition that is the norm in medicine.

We cannot expand the role of home care aides without acknowledging that they intrude to at least some extent on the territory of another occupation—nurses. This long-standing battle plays out in each state since it is at that level that nurse practice acts and scope of practice laws are written and enforced. At a deep level, this struggle reflects the historical tension between the conception of home care aides as providing social service, housekeeping, and companionship versus a view of them as providing medical care.

Sadly, it is not a new insight that modifying the scope of practice is important not just for home care aides but for improving long-term care. In 1996 experts argued that "one task ripe for delegation is dispensing of oral medications. . . . So far a number of states find it easier to create a fiction that many clients—even those with dementia—are self-administering drugs rather than face this issue head on."[16] Over the years since this point was made, numerous experts have argued for expanding the scope of practice for home care aides.[17] Indeed, evaluations of pilot programs that loosen scope of practice restrictions on home care aides find no adverse effects for consumers.[18] Moreover, as already noted, the Cash and Counseling demonstration found no adverse effects in consumer-directed programs with no limitations.

Sometimes the tussle goes well; for example, in Oregon, after what a former Medicaid administrator described as a "slugfest," nurse delegation was loosened.[19] But more typically the battle has been one-sided, since home care aides have few allies and nurses are a powerful group. The story of efforts to create an "advanced home care aide" title in New York illustrates the problem.

Recall that in New York the scope of practice of home care aides is very constrained. The canonical example is the prohibition on them even administering eyedrops; instead, they can only guide the hand of a client toward his or her own eye. Over a decade ago, discussions began around very modestly loosening these restrictions to create an advanced home care aide title. The effort gathered steam in 2012 when Governor Andrew Cuomo's Medicaid Redesign Team recommended creating the title. The idea was quite modest: home care aides would be permitted to administer prepackaged and premeasured medication provided that a supervising nurse had assessed the home care aide's capacity to do this. In fact, to say that the proposed change was minor is an understatement. In New York, home care aides who worked for consumer-directed clients could administer any medicine, as could home care aides in the developmentally disabled system, but regular home care aides could not. There are no such constraints on private-pay home care aides; one such aide I interviewed told me, "I did a lot, helped with the medicine. I measured insulin in the needle. The nurse came and trained you. Say two or three days a week until they see everything is going right. I helped the nurse change bandages."

Legislative approval was needed to change the scope of practice for home care aides, and the relevant legislative committee was responsive to the position of the New York State Nurses Association. In addition, the State Nursing Board—somewhat bizarrely housed in the Department of Education—had to sign off on a training plan. Complicating the politics even further were the vocal disability advocates, who typically oppose any state regulation of scope of practice for home care aides. Finally, the lobby representing home care agencies were players because these agencies had a stake in any change that might increase the compensation they provided to home care aides.

When the proposal was formally introduced in the legislature in the 2013 session, a director of the nurses association testified in melodramatic language that death would follow: "The New York State Nurses Association cannot support proposals that would allow unlicensed assistive personnel to administer medications . . . the ultimate outcome is poorer quality patient care leading to . . . increased patient morbidity, mortality, and cost of care."[20] The proposal was killed that session.

When it was reintroduced the following year, the nurses association, which had other business with the governor, did not oppose the proposal (though they did insist on a ten-to-one ratio of nurses to advanced home care aides). Disability advocates also changed their position because, for complicated reasons, the federal government was holding up a large appropriation that would support consumer-directed programs until the scope of practice was equalized across all New York long-term care programs. Nonetheless, the proposal still did not pass. Advocates believe that two groups killed it. They point out that the State Nursing Board, which had to approve training for advanced home care aides, resisted and worked with legislative allies to stop the idea. They also say there is reason to believe that home care agencies, concerned about increased compensation, also worked to stop the proposal. Making matters even worse, in late 2015 disability advocates withdrew their support for the proposal.

Finally, in 2016, the state legislature enlarged the scope of practice to enable the creation of the advanced home care aide title and the governor signed the legislation in November. Two developments broke the logjam. The Centers for Medicare and Medicaid Services insisted that funds for the Community First Choice demonstration, which was aimed at moving people out of institutions, could not be released until the home care aide scope of practice had been equalized across all populations; since aides working with the developmentally disabled could administer prepoured medicine, this capacity would need to be extended. Second, disabled constituents of the key legislative committee chair were mobilized to put pressure on him to permit the change. Even so, the legislation incorporated extensive, and expensive, nurse supervision, and it is very unclear just how the new title will be implemented.

There are three lessons to be drawn from this saga. The first is that the power and importance of occupational competition cannot be underestimated. Even though the New York Nurses Association eventually softened its initial stance on the proposed change, their opposition continued to be a problem. Second, the obstacles presented by the convoluted nature of bureaucratic politics and regulatory systems cannot be ignored. Finally, old-fashioned partisan legislative politics will stand in the way of change. In the end, even a modest reform to improve opportunities for home care aides fell victim to these forces.

Disarray Among Advocates and Producers Versus Consumers

The different perspectives of the disability advocacy community, public interest advocates, and the elder care community preclude their coming together around a common agenda to upgrade the position of home care aides. Of course, this point can be exaggerated; certainly all of these groups are in favor of more generous funding for Medicaid. But simply putting more money into Medicaid is not likely to be a winning strategy in the foreseeable future. What is needed are structural changes in the role of home care aides, and here the interests diverge.

One aspect of the conflict is the fairly direct divergence of interests between "consumers," who wish to obtain support services as cheaply as possible, and "producers," the home care aides and their advocates who push for improved compensation. A shocking example occurred during oral arguments before the Supreme Court when Justice Stephen Breyer (of the liberal wing of the Court!) questioned whether home care aides should be covered by minimum wage legislation, since doing so would raise the cost for clients:

> If you win this case . . . and I'm worried about this obviously . . . all over the country it's the family . . . who are paying for a companion for an old sick person so they don't have to brought to an institution. . . . It seems to me that there will suddenly be millions of people who are unable to do it . . . and hence millions of sick people who will move to institutions . . . it's a very worrisome point.[21]

This is just a reprise of a long-standing debate about labor standards. After all, if the wages of Wal-Mart employees increase, then diapers might become more expensive for Wal-Mart customers, who typically are lower-income and often in financial distress. It is easy to dismiss these concerns rhetorically; after all, if the goal is to offer the cheapest possible products, then indentured labor is the way to achieve this. But if we get real and move beyond rhetoric, then we must admit that concerns about labor standards are reasonable. Of course, when it comes to long-term care, the ultimate source of this dilemma is the iron cage of Medicaid funding.

This said, the conflict between producers and consumers runs deeper than questions of pricing; it turns on fundamentally different conceptions of the role of home care aides. The disability community strongly opposes any efforts to "medicalize" home care aides or to interpose state regulation between the consumer and the home care aide. These concerns are understandable, but they clash with other reasonable goals—for example, improving the skills of home care aides so that they not only perform better but also have some opportunities for career mobility in health care should they be interested.

An example of this point is found in California, where consumer-directed care dominates and there currently are no training requirements for home care aides. The training arm of the union that represents home care aides, the Service Employees International Union (SEIU), is engaged in a large, federally funded demonstration aimed at testing the impact of increased training on outcomes such as hospital readmissions. Ironically, the level of training being offered in this demonstration is no greater than the minimal training that New York already requires. Nevertheless, the disability community opposed even this very modest initiative. They tried to stop the demonstration grant, and when the advocates of this training asked the state legislature to approve a waiver application to the federal government to expand the demonstration, the disability community blocked it.

In another example, in Massachusetts the Personal Care Attendant Workforce Council, which manages the consumer-directed program, is dominated by disability advocates. This council has rejected any training requirement and also has insisted that the three-hour orientation be conducted by the consumer with no professional present.

The tensions between the two worlds played out dramatically in the case of the Fair Labor Standards Act, which sets the minimum wage and requires overtime payment for covered workers. But who is a covered worker? This is not a trivial question, and it has a long history—for example, in the struggle to provide coverage for farm laborers. The key fight was about the "companionship exemption" in the FLSA, which was intended to exempt babysitters from coverage. (In other words, you do not have to pay your babysitter the minimum wage, nor do you have to offer overtime!) For many years, the U.S. Department of Labor, the agency responsible for administering the FLSA, interpreted the companionship exemption to include home care aides and hence excluded them from FLSA coverage. The fact that home care aides were seen as equivalent to babysitters speaks volumes to one of the underlying challenges to reform.

The Clinton administration tried to reinterpret the exemption and initiated a rule-making process to include home care aides in FLSA coverage, but time ran out and the Bush administration stopped this process. The right of the Department of Labor to include home care aides under the companionship exemption was upheld by the Supreme Court in a 2007 decision.[22] That same year the Fair Home Health Care Act was introduced in the Senate (among its sponsors was Senator Barack Obama), but it never made it out of committee.

The issue was not revisited until five years into the Obama administration, and the Wage and Hours Division again began the process of rule-making to cover home care aides under the FLSA. As the National Employment Law Project argued in its brief, the babysitting image is extremely outdated. Even with their limited scope of practice, home care aides help with ADLs and IADLs, and some provide quasi-medical assistance. Nor is home care a casual business, but rather a large industry with many firms, including profit-making firms. And home care aides are not working for pocket money but rather are adults who support themselves and their families.

Given this logic, and given the Obama administration's renewed commitment to enforcing employment regulations, reinterpreting the companionship exemption made sense. But the challenge lay in the complexity of the long-term care system and the views, legitimate but conflicting, of the relevant parties. Debate and dissent erupted.

The core issue was not the minimum wage, which at $7.25 an hour simply was not binding, but rather three other FLSA requirements: (1) that home care aides be paid overtime, (2) that states in many cases be considered joint employers, and (3) that travel time between jobs be counted as work. The problem with paying home care aides overtime was the impact on state budgets. Consider a home care aide who works twenty hours at one home for one agency and thirty hours at another home for another agency. Neither agency was responsible for overtime pay (ten hours plus travel), but under the new rule the state was. The budgetary implications were substantial, and states, expressing great concern about the proposed rule change, resisted it. Advocates had another worry: if states were made responsible for overtime, they would respond by refusing to permit home care aides to work more than forty hours a week. In the example given here, a different home care aide would be required to work the extra ten hours. A related worry was that the requirement that travel time be compensated would make short-hour cases undesirable and agencies would stop meeting this need.

These complexities are hard to manage in the agency world. There is also the reality that state budgets are constrained and, given the current structure of the industry, the scope for offsetting higher wage costs via higher prices or improved productivity is limited. Even progressive advocates, who never in public would oppose any increase in the minimum wage, expressed concerns in private.

But if there were worries in these sectors, there was outrage in the consumer-directed world, and for understandable reasons. If a relative is caring for you and the state says that she can work for only forty hours, then how do you get more hours if you need them? You are unlikely to have another relative standing by, and so you will have to hire a stranger, yet this is a very uncomfortable solution and one that violates the implicit deal behind consumer-directed care. There were additional concerns that states would respond to their budgetary constraints by undermining *Olmstead,* leading to some degree of reinstitutionalization.

The reaction was fierce. Advocates wrote that, "as hours are capped, disabled people will be forced back into institutions, in violation of their rights. The new rule will have the effect of making home and community based services, and with them, the rights of people with disabilities to live in freedom, an option, not a right." Words were followed with actions, ranging from a letter-writing campaign to a demonstration on the lawn of the labor secretary's house.

It must also be said that advocates in favor of the expanded coverage were tone-deaf and acted as if the entire home care world was agency-directed. One brief in favor of the change said that "narrowing the companionship exemption will not hurt continuity of care. The industry's staggeringly high turnover rates are the greatest threat to continuity of care. Establishing a minimum wage floor will help reduce turnover and improve continuity of care."[23] While this argument was probably true for agencies, it totally missed the point for those in the consumer-directed system. And the Labor Department itself made exactly this error in its report on the economic impact of the new rule.

Not surprisingly, home care agencies also opposed the new regulations (as low-wage employers typically do when minimum wage issues arise) and filed suit. They argued that the Labor Department, in an effort to minimize the impact on casual workers, had written the regulations in a way that inappropriately parsed the workforce into covered and uncovered groups. A district court judge sided with the agencies, but when that ruling was overturned at the appellate level, the Labor Department proceeded to implement the law. In the face of the concerns, however, the department slowed the implementation by, in effect, delaying enforcement for a year and working with states on budget issues. It also issued guidelines for reconciling the new regulations with *Olmstead* requirements. It must be noted, however, that in some states—for example, Massachusetts—the fears of the disability community have been realized: the states have aimed to cap costs by limiting aides to a maximum of forty hours of work a week.[24]

The lesson of this story is not that the extension of minimum wage coverage to home care aides was a mistake. Home care aides are working people who deserve the same protections as others. It is not their fault that the system in which they work is baroquely complicated and that regulations have unexpected consequences. Instead, the lesson is that change is hard in this system, in part because of the system's financial and administrative complexity. But it is also hard because of differences in the needs and perspectives of the clients who are being served as well as differences in how well the relevant players understand each other's views and circumstances.

CONCLUSION

It is easy to understand why the basic situation of home care aides has not changed very much since the New Deal. Public funding for their services comes from a welfare system whose features and political environment block reform. Home care aides are seen as little more than babysitters and housekeepers, and competing occupations frequently block attempts to expand their scope of practice. The two main client groups, the elderly and the disabled, have not been able to come together to demand improvement, and in fact their interests seem to clash. All of this adds up to a recipe for stagnation.

Nevertheless, it is not the end of the story. Shifting demographics will ratchet up pressure to transform the system, some developments in the flow of Medicaid funds offer at least the hope of improvement, and unions, where they are active, can be important advocates for change. These more hopeful trends are the topic of the next chapter.

CHAPTER 9

Forces for Change

Human nature is such that we often find ourselves doing what we have always done simply because it is the easiest thing to do. This is doubly true when it comes to public policy. It takes energy and political capital to change established practices, and often the only reward is making new enemies of those with a vested interest in the status quo. So as a general rule, budgets tend to continue as before, with only small additions or subtractions. Why should the delivery of long-term care be any different? Even accepting the arguments that home care aides can do more and that the system would be improved if they were trained in new skills and permitted to practice them, why would anyone think that it would come to pass? And to dig a deeper hole, what is the basis for expecting that we can overcome the obstacles just laid out?

While caution is always warranted, there are reasons to think that change is possible and that the delivery system for long-term care can be reformed in a way that will offer both better services for the people who need them and better jobs for the people who do the heavy lifting (literally and figuratively).

One driver of change is simple demographics. The demand for long-term care is bound to increase explosively, and the supply of younger people who are willing to do the work may well shrink. Pressures will build to find ways to deliver services, and an element of any solution should be addressing the workforce issues.

The second driver of change, not surprisingly, is financial. Today long-term care costs nearly $300 billion annually, accounting for a large fraction of both insurance expenditures and state budgets (via Medicaid). The ideas laid out here promise to save money through two channels. First, better-quality care delivered by better-trained aides will reduce the toll of chronic illness, the waste of trips to the emergency room, and the use of more expensive nursing homes. Second, this can be achieved by shifting some work to relatively low-paid aides from relatively expensive nurses and other health care professionals.

Trends within the organization of Medicaid, notably the spread of managed care and new approaches to integrating Medicare and Medicaid, offer some reason to believe that incentives can be more properly aligned to move the system in the direction just described. States, which bear much of the financial burden, share in these incentives and also may push for reform.

If all this were to happen, there remains the uncomfortable question of whether home care aides would share in any of the savings achieved through their enhanced role. Who will advocate for home care aides? This brings us to the role of unions. Unions representing home care aides are strong only in a minority of states; these happen to be the biggest states, however, and unions are showing a growing interest in using their power to reconfigure the jobs of home care aides.

DEMOGRAPHICS

Sometimes it seems that employers have an inherent propensity to complain about being unable to find qualified employees. It is certainly true that in any conversation with home health care agencies, one hears complaints about the difficulty of finding home care aides, but these kinds of complaints always have to be treated with caution. Employers across a wide range of industries engage in "cheap talk" about not being able to find people, yet the problem is often just the low wages they offer or their lazy recruiting efforts, and sometimes their complaints are just empty grousing. I ran a small nonscientific experiment in which I advertised (in Massachusetts, a state with a strong job market) for a home care aide to care for my mother and offered $15 an hour. The ad was placed on Care.com, a site that oddly enough also offers help in obtaining babysitters for your children and companions for your pets. That said, over the course of a month I received over thirty responses, and many of the applicants seemed qualified.

But even with a dose of skepticism, it is true that the demand for long-term care will continue to grow, and that if we do not adjust to this it is very unclear who will be there to care for us. Moving beyond this basic point and stating the problem more precisely, however, is considerably more complicated. To do this we need to proceed in several steps:

- The aging of the population will dramatically increase demand for care, but we cannot project just how much demand will grow through population demographics alone; we must also estimate the fraction of the elderly population who will need help based on trends in health status.

- Although much of the popular discussion focuses on the aging of the baby boom generation, in fact about half of the need for long-term care will come from the younger disabled population. Their numbers are large but will not explode, and hence this population's demand for care will moderate the overall rate of increase in demand.

- As we have seen, family and friends provide the bulk of care, but the size of these cohorts will fall relative to the size of the older population. Changes in family structure may also have an impact on the availability of unpaid help.

- Another central concern, the future supply of paid home care aides and CNAs, faces uncertainty, given both the low wages and status of these jobs and the demographic trends, such as the slowing of immigration and the slow growth or nongrowth in the size of the cohort of middle-aged women.

In trying to estimate the coming shortfall of both paid direct care workers and unpaid family members (see appendix D), I have concluded that if the job does not become more attractive, then in the year 2030 there will be a shortage of hundreds of thousands of paid direct care workers and a shortfall of several million unpaid family members. In 2040, the paid direct care shortfall will rise substantially and the family and friends shortfall will be a shocking 11 million. It is important to note that, for reasons I explain later, these are conservative estimates of future shortages.

Some might believe that technology will come to the rescue, and that is certainly a natural thought to have, given all the changes we have witnessed in the past few decades. One important use of technology is in facilitating communications between caregivers and other medical personnel, and a number of demonstration programs do show positive results from innovations along these lines.[1] Fall detectors and emergency response systems are also potentially important, and their utilization is growing.[2] But the bigger question is whether certain innovations, such as robots, will actually reduce the need for caregivers and hence ease prospective shortages.

Thinking about this in a sober-minded way leads to three broad conclusions. First, it is certainly true that over time and in the near future technology will make staying at home easier. Second, technology may transform home care in some distant future, but this will not happen anytime soon. Consider, for example, the ALS technology at the nursing home in Chelsea, Massachusetts, which I described in chapter 7. That system enables paralyzed people to manage their environment to a remarkable degree. But it is also clear that the technology would not work for people with cognitive issues, and as the designer of the system pointed out to me, it would not work in homes because of the need for skilled system maintenance. And third, smaller innovations, such as the use of iPads to record health status or refrigerators that signal when new supplies are needed, will certainly improve care, but they will not change the fundamental nature of care and the need for engaged health care teams and aides. Nor will simple robots that help with chores such as cleaning. This conclusion is supported by a recent careful review of the literature on new technologies and home-based care.[3]

If technology will not solve the problem anytime soon, what will? The solution is to increase the "pull rate"—that is to say, the willingness of people to work as home care aides. Increasing the pull rate will require improving the jobs so that more people are attracted to the work, and one important way to do that is to connect the work of home care aides more tightly to the medical care team in ways that justify improved compensation and offer aides a health care career. Consider the conversation I had with one young woman working as a home care aide:

Aide: Honestly, home health aide is not what I expected it to be. Believe it or not, I actually want to become an RN. I wanted something more in the medical field. . . . I chose the home health aide field. But apparently, I feel like it's more housekeeping and stuff. Even though we do take care of clients, but I feel like it's a mixture of housekeeping, and it's not something I'm learning. So I don't see myself doing this for too long.

Author: I understand. You said you'd like to do something more medical, less housekeeping. If you could rethink this job so you wanted to stay in it, what would it look like?

Aide: More medical stuff like the wound care, being able to put injections and monitor medication.

Author: Do you think you could learn that stuff?

Aide: Of course! That's what I want. That's the field that I'm going for.

Author: When you see the visiting nurses come in, change the dressings and all that, are you thinking, *Hey, I could be doing that?*

Aide: Yeah.

This young woman left her job shortly after our conversation. To attract motivated people like her, the job simply has to be better; if we cannot attract such people, we will be faced with the large shortages outlined earlier. It is reasonable to think that as these shortages become apparent, growing political pressure from aging cohorts will help generate a constituency for change.

MONEY MAKES THE WORLD GO AROUND

The exploding demand for long-term care is putting tremendous pressure on budgets at the state and national levels, and demographic trends will only make the problem worse. These budgetary tensions have led many states to reconfigure their health care systems toward managed care.

The weaknesses of the current system are well known. Under fee-for-service, there are few incentives to be efficient. In addition, expenditures for acute medical care are separated from expenditures for long-term care because the sources of the funding are different. For the approximately 9 million people who are eligible for both programs (so-called duals), Medicare funds their medical care and Medicaid is responsible for their long-term care. One consequence of not unifying these expenditures (or, in economist-speak, not "internalizing" the costs) is that long-term care providers, bearing no responsibility for the cost of medical services, have no incentives to economize on medical costs. As mentioned earlier, one common result is that these providers instruct their home care aides to call 911 and send clients to emergency rooms even when such action is not warranted. The implication of this system is that there is little to be gained from training home care aides in skills that could reduce medical costs (for instance, by limiting ER visits, reducing rehospitalization, and alleviating chronic conditions) because the payers and providers of long-term care do not benefit from these savings.

Partly as a result of this thinking and partly (and more likely) because of a broad perception (fairly or unfairly) that there is "fat" in the system, states are moving toward managed care systems. In managed care, an insurance company (the managed care organization, or MCO) receives a capitated payment for each client and out of that payment is responsible for providing medical care, care coordination, and support services.

The simplest—and to date most common—version of managed care ignores the issue of duals and the inconsistent incentives facing Medicare and Medicaid and instead simply rolls Medicaid-supported long-term care into a managed care system. This approach has spread rapidly across the country.[4]

Under this simpler, long-term-care-only version, the managed care insurance company is responsible only for home care, nursing homes, or other alternatives such as adult day centers. In some states, the insurance firm is also expected to assess the needs of the client and provide care coordination, while in other states an independent agency does this. This flavor of managed care moves partly in the direction of getting the incentives right. Most importantly, the insurance company is incentivized to keep people out of expensive nursing homes and instead pay for the provision of care at home. In principle, this incentive should lead insurance firms to value the services of home care aides to the extent that high-performing aides can reduce the chances of nursing home admission. However, insurance firms have no incentive to reduce acute medical expenditures since these are not included in the capitation payment.

The second version of managed care includes Medicare expenditures on acute care as well as Medicaid spending on support services. Considering how much the 9 million duals cost the system, these fully integrated managed care models that include both Medicaid and Medicare are important because they get all the incentives rights.[5] An insurance company will want not just to keep people out of nursing homes but also to keep people healthy and out of hospitals.

There are two major challenges facing these fully integrated or dual managed care models. The first is that they are very hard to operate, because integrating Medicare and Medicaid is difficult bureaucratically. The integration of the two programs raises the management bar considerably in terms of effective assessment and care coordination as well as high-quality delivery of both medical and long-term care. The second complication is that while states can mandate managed care for long-term services, federal law prohibits requiring Medicare recipients to join managed care. People can be enrolled, but they have the opportunity to opt out, and therefore take-up of these models has been halting.

The first two fully integrated managed care programs were implemented in Minnesota and Massachusetts, both well over a decade ago. Today the federal government is supporting demonstrations in six states, although enrollment remains limited.[6] That said, there is considerable momentum and interest behind these programs.

Managed Care and the Role of Home Care Aides

Managed care is relatively new to the arena of long-term services and supports, and with the exceptions of Minnesota, Massachusetts, and Arizona, it is brand-new with respect to the integration of Medicare and Medicaid. Some observers are skeptical about managed care largely on the grounds that most insurance companies have limited experience with long-term care and hence there may well be a lengthy learning period before we see any benefits. This point became concrete when I interviewed several managed care firms about their programs and asked how they worked with home care agencies; it was quickly apparent that they did not know the landscape. One insurance company manager said of her own organization, "We just don't get it." A home care agency leader told me that she dealt with thirty managed care organizations and only two were willing to discuss strategies for improving delivery. Yet another agency head complained that the managed care organizations with which she dealt did not understand care coordination and that she had to fight to get reimbursed for sending nurses to her clients' homes. To be fair, a survey of long-term care clients in California's managed care program found that nearly 80 percent reported themselves satisfied with services that were the same as or better than those offered in the prior fee-for-service system.[7]

There are also worries in the disability community that insurance companies have limited experience with consumer-directed programs and that care coordinators find enrolling people in consumer-directed programs to be both uncomfortable and too much work. Indeed, disability advocates attribute the slow growth of consumer-directed enrollment to the reluctance of MCOs to support the model.[8] These concerns were reinforced by the conclusion reached by a federal survey of the impact on consumer-directed programs of managed care in five states: "Even states with a historical commitment to participant direction leave the future growth . . . to the discretion of MCOs (which may or may not be committed to such growth)."[9]

Advocates are also worried. Legal assistance organizations report incidents of long-term managed care firms cherry-picking clients by making it hard for those with severe needs to enroll, dis-enrolling expensive patients, deliberately making it difficult to reach anyone with whom to appeal enrollment decisions, and assessing clients for inappropriately low levels of care.[10] Recent lawsuits against managed care companies in Tennessee and New York speak to these worries.[11]

Managed care organizations argue that over time, as the system rationalizes, they will turn more directly to issues of quality and care coordination. Some evidence in support of this perspective comes from evaluations of managed care in states that have had longer experience in long-term managed care, notably Massachusetts and Minnesota. (I discuss the lessons from these states later in the chapter.) There are also less obvious benefits. Home care is characterized by numerous small "mom-and-pop" agencies that are hard to monitor and whose internal systems leave much to be desired. The spread of managed care is likely to lead to a shakeout in this industry, with larger, better managed, and more efficient agencies winning and obtaining a larger share of the market.

All this said, a well-functioning system of managed care would not only overcome the "you are on your own" nature of fee-for-service but also create incentives to upgrade the role of home care aides. Managed care payment systems may give insurance companies a good reason to upgrade the work of home care aides because theoretically they will have an incentive to look for the most cost-effective way to deliver quality care, and making greater use of a large low-wage workforce fits this strategy. This incentive will lead them to rethink the contribution of home care aides and to expand their role. Home care aides can be better trained at their current range of tasks, and if even some of the work of more expensive practitioners, such as nurses, physical therapists, and dietitians, can be taken up by home care aides, then all the better from the insurance company's perspective. Put differently, home care aides engage in activities that should be of considerable interest to managed care organizations.

Senior Care Options (SCO), the Massachusetts dual managed care program, enrolls just under 40,000 clients. According to a recent report, the model incorporates many of the best practice ideas in currency: care coordination, attention to transitions, and a person-centered system aimed at the full range of issues—medical, behavioral, social—confronting clients.[12] The results seem to bear this out.[13]

All of this is good, but what about the home care aides? Here the story is disappointing. I interviewed managers at three of the five SCO insurance companies, and each told the same story: yes, it would make sense to broaden the scope of home care aides' work, but no, we do not do this.

All three of the insurance companies outsourced hiring and assigning home care aides to agencies, and hence they were not fully engaged in the work of the home care aides. Two of the insurance companies simply had not thought about utilizing home care aides, despite the fact that one of them did health coaching utilizing a peer coaching model developed at Stanford. The third insurance company was committed to health coaching but assigned the role to nurses. The nurses saw patients every three or six months, but the organization saw no role for home care aides in reinforcing what the nurses taught clients, despite the fact that the aides were with the clients every day. Because none of the companies had written performance contracts with the agencies, their leverage was limited. Added evidence of reluctance to reconsider the role of home care aides came from the union representing them, SEIU's 1199, which reported that it had developed a position paper outlining an "enhanced home care aide" role but was unable to get any of the SCOs interested in the idea.

Each company offered different explanations for ignoring home care aides. One senior manager said that agencies were difficult to work with because they were fragmented and unsophisticated. "Sometimes there isn't even someone to talk to." "Hard to sort the good and the bad." Another cited logistical issues: if home care aides were trained in higher-order skills but these were not needed for all clients, how could scheduling be managed? A third firm was the source of the comment that home care aides were "minimum-wage people" and hence presumably unable to do more.

Green Shoots

The foregoing raises a hard question: although it might be true in theory that managed care, particularly fully integrated managed care, creates incentives to better utilize home care aides, are the incentives too weak and the reality simply not consistent with theory? This certainly would not be the first time that theory was dismissed by the "real world." Happily, there are some examples— some "green shoots"—that suggest otherwise.

PACE (Program of All-inclusive Care for the Elderly) is a Medicare-Medicaid option, written into the law, for adults ages fifty-five and older. It grew from the On Lok Senior Health Services Program in San Francisco, founded in 1971. "On lok" means "peaceful happy abode" in Cantonese. These programs receive a capitation (per person) payment that covers all services. Programs have their own caregiving staff, covering a wide range of areas, and revolve around an adult day center. Enrollees may live at home, in a nursing home, or in a smaller residence for frail adults, but they typically spend their days at the center and receive all their care from the program or the program's network of specialists.

PACE has grown slowly, and there is some debate about why that is. Certainly, the capital costs involved in establishing a program are considerable. In addition, clients need to be willing to give up their own established network of care providers and commit to the PACE system. On the other hand, the mantra of care coordination is more fully implemented in PACE than anywhere else. Whether PACE saves money or leads to better health outcomes is disputed in the literature.[14]

For our purposes, the question is whether a long-established, fully integrated model that creates just the kind of incentives described here leads to a broader role for home care aides. (Sadly, as in all else, this question is not even raised in the evaluation literature on PACE.) The answer is yes.

At the core of the PACE model is the interdisciplinary care team (IDT), which consists, by regulation, of eleven categories of caregivers (doctors, nurses, physical therapists, social workers, and so on), and one of these categories is home care aides. The team meets each morning and reviews the status of the patients. At the three PACE programs with which I am familiar, home care aides are fully involved and participate in these meetings. Indeed, when I attended an IDT meeting at the East Boston Neighborhood Health Center's PACE program, it began with a home care aide reporting to the group on a difficulty that one of her patients was having with her medicines. At another PACE center, the home care aides meet with the IDT only once a week, but the aides at this center reported that this is the first time in their career that anyone has paid any attention at all to them. At the third program, home care aides attend meetings and go to medical appointments with their clients. All three programs provide home care aides with additional training (on topics such as nutrition and infection control) beyond the requirements for the home health home care aide or certified nursing assistant title. The programs are also considering an expansion of the role of home care aides to include health coaching and, in one case, assisting physical therapists.

PACE programs have a small footprint, but the federal government recently opened the door to for-profit providers to build centers and receive reimbursement. The PACE Innovation Act of 2015 additionally authorizes pilot programs to extend the PACE model to a broader population than is currently allowed.[15] There are also indications that private equity finance is interested; if this happens, scale may increase and the demonstration effect of an enhanced role for aides may be stronger.[16]

Finally, insurance companies are not the only player with a growing financial interest in finding more efficient ways to deliver long-term care. The burden on state budgets is substantial, and thoughtful state players should push to expand the role of home care aides for all the reasons laid out here.

Indeed, the broader health care system is undergoing a series of reorganizations that will push it toward finding ways to deliver quality care using a less expensive mix of personnel. One of these changes is experimentation with accountable care organizations (ACOs). An ACO is a provider—typically a hospital or medical practice—that cuts out the insurance company and assumes at least some of the risk for patient health. Hence, like PACE programs, an ACO is fully capitated. These models were encouraged by the Affordable Care Act of 2010, and there are a few in operation.

It is not yet clear whether the ACO model will catch on, in part because it has been slow to diffuse and in part because the future of the ACA itself is not clear. However, the central idea—that large anchor institutions, such as hospitals, should organize care in their catchment area and bear some risk—is in fact likely to spread. This possibility is apparent in pressures from the Medicare system and also in the range of Medicaid redesign initiatives in many states.

One example is New York's Mount Sinai Hospital, which I described earlier. Mount Sinai is engaged in an initiative called the Hospital Home Care Collaborative, one of the options that the state offers as part of its Medicaid redesign push. The Collaborative aims to deploy a team-based model with a clear role for home care aides as part of the care team.[17] Over time the idea is for Mount Sinai to move to full risk-based contracting for the population in its catchment area. Planning includes working with home health care agencies and the SEIU local representing home care aides to train people in the skills needed to execute the model. The vision for home care aides includes both more active "eyes and ears" communication and health coaching.

The bottom line is that there are indeed reasons to be optimistic that new financing approaches and public policy initiatives will create incentives to upgrade the work of home care aides. Again, however, it is important to be realistic. It is hard for programs to fully involve home care aides in more advanced roles because, as one director pointed out to me, coordination and management issues get in the way. When dealing with frail and needy populations, unexpected problems often arise, and hence scheduling home care aides to do "extra" activities, like health coaching or assistance with physical therapy, can be difficult. Scheduling can also be hard: providing home care aides with full-time work may involve having some highly trained home care aides spend some of their time in settings that do not require their skills, and this raises issues around compensation. Additionally, while I have argued strenuously that many home care aides are eager to take on these tasks, it would be naive to think that all aides are interested or capable; hence, care would be required in selection and training.

These qualifications are real and must be respected. But they do not undermine the main point: with proper incentives, the role of many home care aides can be expanded, with considerable benefits to all parties.

UNIONS

States and managed care companies have some incentive to push for change, but as we have seen, their incentives are purely self-interested—they have no interest in home care aides per se. Nor does the current state of play suggest that they are rethinking the delivery of long-term care yet. By contrast, unions that represent home care aides have a direct interest in improving the job. In addition, at least in principle, unions represent the answer to another question: Even if the job of home care aides is expanded, and even if they begin to save the medical care system a substantial amount of money in the delivery of long-term care, will home care aides themselves benefit? What will keep payers from simply taking the gains and not sharing them? That this is not a trivial concern is shown in research on the Green House nursing homes (discussed in chapter 7). Although the CNAs in these models did a good deal more than CNAs in traditional settings, their compensation did not differ significantly.[18] Again, we should be able to look to unions to answer this concern. (The demographics of supply and demand should also help.)

Unions play an additional role that is not typically considered when economists and policy wonks add up the pluses and minuses: they operate politically at the state level to protect and, to some extent, expand Medicaid budgets.

Set against this optimistic view of the potential for unions are several concerns. The first is simply that unions are a force only in a few states—notably New York, California, Washington, Illinois, Oregon, and Massachusetts. To make matters worse, a recent Supreme Court decision threatens to undermine union power in the West Coast states, and possibly in Illinois and Massachusetts as well. Additionally, where they are strong, unions have clearly succeeded in raising hourly wages, but they have not had as great an impact on annual earnings because employers have a lever they can use to adjust to higher wages—namely, lower hours. An additional complication is that in some states unions represent nursing home workers and hospital workers as well as home care aides, and it sometimes appears that the home care aides are at the bottom of the list of union priorities, just as they are with other actors in the system.

My bottom line is that while it is reasonable to be critical of some aspects of union policy, on balance unions are clearly a force for good in the industry and should be supported. Given their limited range and the challenges of new organizing, they are probably not the primary answer—but they are certainly part of the solution.

The Strong Presence of Unions in the Health Care Industry

Unions in the United States have been on the retreat: the percentage of private-sector workers covered by contracts now stands at around 7 percent, and the attack on public-sector unions that was initiated by Governor Scott Walker in Wisconsin has spread and been given momentum by the Supreme Court. There is a lively discussion about what it might take to turn this trend around and about the promise of alternative models of employee voice, such as worker centers or mobilizations such as the "Fight For Fifteen" campaign. But health care is something of an exception to the trend, with an increasing union membership rate and a growing number of union elections.[19]

Union activity among home care aides has also been growing, with large powerful unions in New York, California, Washington, and Oregon and growing strength in Massachusetts, Vermont, and Minnesota. Nationally, about 600,000 home care aides are represented by either the SEIU or the American Federation of State, County, and Municipal Employees (AFSME). The density of representation of home care aides is uneven across the country (the majority of the represented workers are in California, and New York comes in second), but overall representation is larger than is the case for most low-wage work.

The history of these unions for home care aides has been well told in depth elsewhere.[20] Here it is relevant that when the 1199 local of SEIU organized agencies in New York, the process was facilitated by the fact that the agencies were subcontractors to the city government and hence not in a position to resist once the city agreed to union representation. On the West Coast, with the consumer-directed model, organizing was very difficult, since home care aides were isolated in clients' homes and it was unclear with whom the union could negotiate. The breakthrough came with the idea of creating a state- (or county-) level authority to be the employer of record and hence a bargaining partner for the union. Once these authorities were created (the first was in San Mateo in 1993), the SEIU was successful in signing up home care aides.

The Impact of Unions on Compensation

It is very hard to come to any other conclusion than that unions raise wages of people at the bottom of the job market. For example, in private-sector service jobs that are unionized, the hourly wage is nearly 60 percent higher than it is in non-union jobs.[21] The gains from unionization persist after controlling for workers' demographic characteristics and conducting finer-grained industry breakdowns.

It is clear that, with respect to hourly wages, home care aides benefit from organization. In Massachusetts, SEIU recently succeeded in signing a contract with the state that raises wages to $15.00 an hour by 2018 (but without benefits). In New York City, the negotiated contract is $11.00 an hour plus $4.09 in benefits, while in Washington State the top of the scale is $15.00 an hour. In addition, in New York the union recently achieved so-called wage parity, which equalized the wages of the two subcategories of home care aides: home health home care aides and personal care assistants.

In most industries, employers can increase their capital investments in response to wage increases and hence reduce the amount of labor they use. Just how much this happens is hotly debated, with opponents of unions arguing that this response undermines any apparent economic gains. Most scholars would say that, even taking this response into account, employees generally are better off if organized by unions. But in long-term care the situation is more complicated. The issue is not capital substitution but rather how many hours of care are allocated to consumers. Adjusting hours is much easier than adding more equipment, and so it is possible that changes in assigned hours offset wage gains.

When we look at annual earnings (using the 2015 American Community Survey) and compare union to non-union states, the story is somewhat complicated. The union looks good for home care aides in New York, where median annual earnings are $18,023. On the other hand, in unionized California median earnings are $14,018 (but with benefits, which is important), but this does not compare favorably with non-union Florida's median annual earnings of $18,023. Of course, in other non-union states the numbers are worse. For example, for Ohio median earnings are $15,019.

Non-Wage Impacts of Unions

As we have seen, the Medicaid system is an iron cage that limits what is possible both for clients and for those who provide services. Unions can deploy their political power to pressure governors and legislators to appropriate more money, and each state where unions are strong can provide examples of the effectiveness of this pressure. In New York in 1988, for instance, the SEIU local 1199 and Governor Mario Cuomo (father of the current governor) increased state funding for home care, and this pattern continued in 2002 with the Republican governor, George Pataki, and on to Governor Andrew Cuomo, with whom the union has been a full participant in discussions around Medicaid redesign.

Unions are also occasionally active on the issues at the center of this book: expanding the scope of practice for home care aides. In New York, the union was one of the major advocates for the advanced home care aide title. In both California and Washington State, the fact that the unions have obtained large federal demonstration grants to experiment with extended training (or any training at all in California!) suggests that the role of home care aides will be extended. In Massachusetts, the local chapter of SEIU 1199 has pushed to have home care aides play a role in care coordination in managed dual programs by being empowered to communicate with the care team and trained to recognize warning signs. The union also has sought changes in nurse practice acts to permit medication administration and physical training assistance.

Related to this union activity on behalf of home care aides is the important fact that unions in Massachusetts, New York, and Washington State operate large training funds (financed through negotiations with state Medicaid authorities) that could be used to train home care aides for expanded roles or career paths into other occupations.

Worries About Union Involvement

No institution is perfect: on the other side of the ledger are legitimate concerns about the performance of the unions representing home care aides. One broad worry stems from SEIU's strategy of creating massive locals in order to have the heft to confront large national health care corporations. For example, the locals in New York and Massachusetts are part of a huge unit that operates along most of the East Coast. Although these locals are powerful, their very size makes it hard for them to be fully participatory from the viewpoint of members, and there is a strong top-down flavor to them. Observers who are broadly sympathetic to unions have expressed significant concerns, and conflicts around this strategy have led to bitter internecine struggles on the West Coast.[22]

There are other less global worries. In New York, the local includes hospital workers and CNAs in nursing homes as well as home health home care aides, and home care aides sometimes seem to be relegated to the bottom of the union hierarchy, just as they are more broadly in the health care system. More money and more jobs are at stake for the union in the other sectors, and this naturally can affect priorities, both with respect to the attention paid to home care aides and in policymaking. For example, of the thousands of home care aides who are trained through the New York training fund every year, only a few hundred are in career path programs; the rest simply take the mandatory annual twelve hours of service training that the state Medicaid program requires. Additionally, little effort is made to move home care aides into the other health care jobs that fall under the union ambit. By contrast, the union training fund in Washington State is considerably more ambitious on behalf of the home care aides it serves.

Challenges Facing Unions

As the foregoing suggests, not all is positive on the union front, and in some respects the performance of unions with respect to home care aides has been disappointing. But that is not the main headline. It seems clear that home care aides are better off if they belong to a union, and it also seems clear that unions are a constituency interested in pushing for a more expansive role for home care aides in the health care and long-term care systems. But home care aides' unions are finding themselves in a difficult political environment and in some respect face existential challenges.

Outside of states with consumer-directed programs—where unions have succeeded by using their political clout to have the state establish a health care authority with which they can bargain—the record of unions in organizing agencies is mixed. In New York, little progress has been made in recent years in signing up new agencies. An additional sign of the problem appears in Massachusetts, where 1199 has succeeded in organizing its consumer-directed home care aides using the same tools as in California—signing a contract with the state—but at the time of this writing has organized only one agency. Again by contrast, in Washington State SEIU has achieved density in both the agency and individual contractor worlds.

Adding to the challenge is the broad reorganization in health care systems, which threatens the employment base of unions beyond the world of home care aides. Medicaid redesign, undertaken by every state in order to save money and (perhaps) improve quality, is forcing hospitals to shrink and merge. These changes pose major challenges to health care unions, which are understandably interested in protecting the jobs of their members and maintaining union density. At best, the widespread reorganization of health care systems distracts unions from thinking about how to improve the jobs of the workers who tend to be on the bottom of the health care totem pole (home care aides).

These challenges are serious enough, but even more ominous is a recent Supreme Court decision that threatens to cut the feet from under unions in consumer-directed states. At issue were the automatic dues payments built into union contracts. The logic of the so-called check-off is that unions represent all employees and hence have a right to discourage free-riding. The Supreme Court had held automatic dues payments to be legal in the case of public employees in general (in the famous *Abood v. Detroit Board of Education* case). This arrangement was challenged by union adversaries, who argued that the real employer under consumer direction is each client (who can hire and fire) and that the mandatory dues check-off therefore violated freedom of speech. Those in favor of maintaining the dues check-off pointed to the broad public interest in a quality long-term care workforce and the benefits of union-management cooperation. The Supreme Court in 2015 agreed, however, with the other side: in *Harris v. Quinn,* it held that mandatory dues check-off for these "quasi-public" employees was unconstitutional. As a result, unions in the affected states will have to organize members one by one in order to maintain membership and collect dues. It is not clear how feasible this effort will be, but even if it is possible, it will certainly use up energy and resources and detract from more creative work.

In additional bad news, court decisions or policies by hostile governors in some unionized states have also set back unions representing aides. In Michigan, Governor Rick Snyder issued an executive order in 2012 denying consumer-directed aides a dues check-off, and an effort to overturn this order via a referendum to amend the state constitution failed. In 2016, the highest court in Pennsylvania held that the state labor relations act excluded home health workers from collective bargaining, and it overturned an executive order by Democratic governor Tom Wolf that granted union representation to aides.

CONCLUSION

There are plenty of reasons to be pessimistic about initiatives to upgrade the role of home care aides and improve their wages and other aspects of their jobs in the process. Most fundamental is the persistent image of home care aides as poor women, often of color and frequently immigrants, whose work amounts to not much more than babysitting and whose employment is a form of welfare. Senior policymakers would never admit to these views, but surely their benign neglect of home care aides and the absence of serious investments in demonstrations aimed at searching for better practices speak volumes. And sad to say, it is in the interest of competing occupations to reinforce this image.

Beyond these optics are more tangible sources of concern. Medicaid is an iron cage whose financial constraints limit innovation and whose wide variation in policies across states makes reform difficult.

But there is hope. It is in the interest of three important constituencies to change this picture. First, and most importantly, the exploding demand for long-term care on the not-too-distant horizon and the declining availability of unpaid family supports will have America's middle class looking more and more to home care aides. Attracting more people to this field is likely to require enlarging the job and increasing the wages. More directly, if people want high-quality help, then additional training will be important. Second, both states and insurance companies, notably managed care organizations, should come to the realization that they can save money if home care aides have broader responsibilities. And certainly advocates, including unions, will continue to push for better jobs.

So there are reasons for optimism, but it remains unclear whether they will all come together. It is not impossible that the system will continue to mud-dle through. Significant change will happen, in my view, only if policymakers wake up to the issues and jump-start that change. It will also require that those who would benefit from progress, consumers themselves, set aside their disagreements and organize politically. Just what all of this means is the topic of the next and final chapter.

CHAPTER 10

Moving Forward

The logic laid out in this book is straightforward. Today America's elderly and disabled citizens are cared for by a low-wage and poorly trained workforce. Continuing in this way is in no one's interest, and the case is compelling to transform the jobs of direct care workers.

My case rests on multiple legs. The growing demand for long-term care will require a larger workforce, but projections indicate shortages of workers and we cannot attract more people unless direct care jobs are expanded and conditions improved. Expanding the jobs will have other important benefits. It will improve care through multiple channels: by better addressing chronic conditions, easing transitions between hospitals and home, and facilitating communication and information-sharing with other members of care teams. In addition, expanding the job will save money by reducing unneeded emergency room and hospital visits and limiting the use of nursing homes. Shifting some tasks to direct care workers, who are lower-paid employees, will also save money. The result is a virtuous circle in which improving the jobs helps pay for itself.

In short, expanding direct care jobs is in the interest of consumers because direct care workers will be available and will do a better job. Expanding the job is also in the interest of the industry and the payers—the insurance companies and governments—because it will save them money. The challenge lies in making this case more broadly understood and engaging in the political action to make it happen.

The challenge of enlarging the job of direct care workers, treating them with dignity, and rewarding their work touches on another challenge facing the nation: successfully addressing the unequal outcomes throughout the job market. A subtext of this book has been the argument that improving job quality and reducing the size of the low-wage job market requires that we go beyond rhetoric and calls for fairness and instead dive into the weeds of specific industries and occupations. This is as true for the long-term care industry as it is for other low-wage industries. We need to understand the incentives and constraints facing employers, employees, and policymakers and to think creatively about reconfiguring the system so that the incentives shift and point to better outcomes for the workforce.

OUR LONG-TERM CARE "SYSTEM"

The first point to be made about long-term services and supports is that we do not take it seriously as a problem or as a system. This may seem odd and totally wrong to people who work hard to deliver services, and it may also seem bizarre given the amount of money that is spent on them. But think about the indicators. There are no national training standards for home care aides (outside of Medicare, which numerically is not important when it comes to home care aides), even though they are central to the quality of care. Gerontology as a specialty is at the bottom of the medical hierarchy (as measured by pay), there are very few new specialists in training, and there are no required medical school courses for residents in other specialties.[1] The Affordable Care Act called for a workforce commission on long-term care, but it was never established. Our delivery system is an impenetrable hodgepodge that even experts have trouble coherently describing.

The "system" is remarkably difficult from the perspective of those in need and their families. Can they stay at home or is a nursing home the best choice? If a nursing home is needed, how can a good one be identified? If the person in need can stay at home, how is a caregiver found? Should the person in need use an agency? Or perhaps a clearinghouse such as a web-based service, or a registry, or an informal network? Should family or friends be paid to provide care? How should they be paid? Through Medicaid or insurance, or out of pocket?

As those in need and their families face these hard problems, we also know that the health care system is changing in dramatic ways. Health care providers are increasingly being rewarded on results rather than procedures. The delivery of care itself is being disrupted—for example, by the walk-in clinics, or "docs in a box," that are proliferating in city storefronts and in pharmacies.[2] Moreover, technology giants such as IBM increasingly see health care as ripe for improvement via the application of data mining and analysis.[3]

What is odd about all of this is that while the country is thinking deeply about how to reform health care delivery, little attention is paid to our LTSS system. Efforts to rethink and improve LTSS are not only minor relative to numerous innovations in the provision of acute care but also invisible in national political debates regarding health care reform. Making this neglect of the issue even more mystifying is the fact that long-term care is enormously costly (over $300 billion in expenditures, plus the enormous implicit cost of unpaid family assistance); in addition, only brief reflection is needed to be convinced that the quality of people's lives is dramatically dependent on the quality of the long-term care they receive.

A moment's thought about the points just made shows the complexities and contradictions. If care is too expensive, then perhaps we should keep the wages of caregivers low, since any improvement will only make the problem harder for families. Yet as implacable demographics ratchet up the demand for care, how will we find a workforce adequate to meet that demand if these are lousy jobs? And most importantly, if we want the best for people in need, do we really think an army of low-paid and poorly trained caregivers will provide it?

We can think about this point in another way. Consider the lively national debate over public education over the past several decades, as well as the extensive innovation and investment in new ideas. Now compare this level of attention to what we give to long-term care. It is not even close. The attention gap is disconcerting given the number of people whose quality of life is at stake.

A recent example of this neglect can be found in the aftermath of the only recent large-scale home care demonstration, the Personal and Home Care Aide State Training (PHCAST) program, which ran from 2010 to 2012 and funded training innovations in six states. These interventions were not conducted consistently across the states, the evaluators relied on state reporting of outcomes and collected no independent data, trainee experience and turnover were not consistently measured across the states, and no data were collected on the impact of increased training on client outcomes.[4] A similar story emerges from a recent General Accountability Office (GAO) examination of how the federal government monitors client outcomes and safety in long-term care. The GAO reported that both the data collection and the attention paid to the issue were haphazard.[5]

In thinking about why home care is so neglected, two explanations stand out. The first is the range of attitudinal challenges that I have emphasized. Aides are held in very low regard, expectations of what they can accomplish are minimal, and long-term care is seen as a dead end that holds little interest to the medical community. Countering this explanation is the second: the delivery system is unbelievably complex, with multiple programs with their own rules and with every state doing things differently. Given the complexity of this "system," one must have some sympathy for the federal officials trying to get their arms around it and move it forward.

Delivery Is Beyond Complicated

Our system for providing long-term care in this country is complicated and often impossible to understand—impossible for the consumers who need the care, impossible for the providers, and impossible for the policymakers and payers.

There are two systems of long-term care: unpaid family and friends and paid home care aides. The family-and-friends system is by far the largest, but it places significant strain on caregivers and we as a nation do very little to support them. Furthermore, the unpaid system is connected to the paid system via consumer-directed care, which does compensate family members but is available only under Medicaid.

The second system, paid assistance, is chopped up into many pieces. Medicaid is an income-tested welfare program, but middle- and working-class people can sometimes find ways to enroll in it if they play the game right.[6] And Medicaid is not really a system: the rules vary across states, and even at the federal level each of a plethora of subprograms has its own rules. Medicare does not pay for extended long-term care, but clients and their families often see it as a component of the overall long-term care system because it covers home and nursing home care after hospital discharge. Finally, in addition to

Medicaid and Medicare, there is a panoply of much smaller federal initiatives, many of which are funded under the Older Americans Act of 1965, as well as occasional state-funded efforts. These programs can be important for people (who may depend on, for instance, Meals on Wheels) but are not significant in size and reach.

The delivery system for paid care reflects the fragmented nature of the payment system. There is, of course, the divide between consumer-directed programs and agency-based care. Among agencies, some are purely Medicaid providers, some mix Medicaid and Medicare, some add private pay to their Medicaid/Medicare portfolio, and some only handle private pay. In addition, many families obtain paid care through informal networks.

It is not hard to imagine that the quality of care varies across these segments, and this brings us to another fundamental characteristic of our "system": it is income-stratified, and in a very odd way. If you are poor enough to qualify for Medicaid, you can obtain paid services, and if you are wealthy enough to pay out of pocket or buy long-term care insurance, you too are in reasonable shape. But if you are in the vast middle, you are on your own (unless you can maneuver into Medicaid coverage).

The delivery system for long-term care is so opaque and difficult to understand—much less navigate—that a new profession, geriatric care manager, has emerged to help people manage it. Geriatric care managers help find providers and financing when long-term care is needed, but they are paid privately and are available only to a tiny slice of our citizens. The rapid growth of this profession is what scholars call an "unobtrusive indicator" of a problem: making sense of long-term care, finding help, and paying for it are challenges beyond the capacity of most of us.

The Politics Make It Worse

As we think about constructive steps to improving long-term care, the politics becomes problematic. One core issue is that Medicaid, the dominant payer, is fundamentally a welfare program. This has several implications. There is little broad-based support for funding Medicaid adequately even though, ironically, working- and middle-class people sometimes find ways to utilize it. Second, as with many welfare programs, Medicaid administration is decentralized to the states, and hence the rules vary and national policy is difficult to achieve. Finally, funding for Medicaid has to compete with funding for other, more popular, state programs.

The second political problem is internal to the broader medical system. Scope of practice restrictions and occupational rivalries impede efforts to enlarge the role of home care aides and other personnel in ways that might lead to better outcomes for all parties. Furthermore, long-term care is not well understood and often not respected by medical professionals.

The third problem is attitudinal. I have documented extensively the lack of respect for direct care workers and the reluctance to see them as potential contributors to health care teams. These low expectations make it difficult to expand their role.

The ultimate challenge is the lack of broad support for change. The differing perspectives of disability advocates and advocates for the elderly with respect to training standards and career paths for home care aides make it hard to build a coalition for reform. But the problem is deeper: there is huge and growing demand for services that are unevenly and inequitably distributed, and it is the middle classes who are the hardest hit. The financial pressures will only grow worse. Yet, despite all of this, there is no real political movement to reform the system comparable to, say, the civil rights movement, the educational reform movement, the gay rights movement, or the environmental movement. Long-term care is a silent crisis.

WHERE DO WE GO FROM HERE?

The focus of this book has been on paid direct care workers—the home care aides and CNAs who have a dramatic impact on the quality of life and quality of care for consumers on a day-to-day basis. Anyone with an elderly parent or disabled child who needs help will testify to this effect.

There are three steps along the path to achieving the goal of improving these jobs. The first step is to demonstrate that direct care workers can in fact perform well in expanded roles and that allowing them to do so will attract the workforce we need, improve care, and save the system money. The second step is to establish a system for training them for these roles. And the third step is to think through the politics of making it happen.

The preceding chapters have provided the evidence regarding performance. As I have demonstrated, direct care workers are disrespected and devalued, key public officials know very little about the actual delivery of long-term care or the role of aides, doctors and nurses do not include them as part of care teams, and insurance companies pay little if any attention to the direct care workforce. But these attitudes do not reflect what is possible.

I showed in chapter 4 that broader jobs would attract a larger workforce and reduce turnover. In chapter 7, I laid out in detail the evidence that direct care workers could do a great deal more and that if they were allowed to do so, not only would outcomes for clients improve but the health care system would save considerable money. These savings would come in part from reducing avoidable costs associated with chronic illnesses, such as unnecessary emergency room visits, hospitalizations, or nursing home stays due in part to poorly managed transitions out of hospitals. Well-trained and empowered aides could help with these issues. The other source of savings is having home care aides do some of the work of higher-paid health care personnel, who could then work "at the top of their license" instead of at the bottom.

What would it take to enlarge the role of home care aides in order to achieve these benefits and savings?

A Framework for Improving Jobs and Care

Over the last several decades, a substantial amount of thought has gone into the question of how to nudge employers to follow what has been termed the high road when it comes to their workforce. The term "high road" refers to a bundle of practices—a commitment to training, utilizing the workforce's ideas and empowering them to improve production and quality, decent compensation, and voice—that define good employers and, importantly, profitable and high-quality production systems.

These ideas have been applied and disseminated in a wide range of industries, including low-wage service jobs. A useful frame for our discussion here is to apply this way of thinking to long-term care. The first step in proceeding logically down this path is to ask for what I have termed "existence proofs"— evidence that aides can perform effectively in broader roles and examples of employers that have successfully implemented high-road practices. The second step is to discern the characteristics of these employers and determine whether they are generalizable. The final step is to ask what combination of carrots and sticks will lead to a broader dissemination of this approach.

As things stand today, the high road is clearly narrow and short. This brings us to the central question: How do we incentivize a broader diffusion of high-road practices? What combination of evidence and incentives can turn the tide? In focusing on incentives, I depart from discussions that focus entirely on a fairness argument. I agree that home care aides—and other low-wage workers—are treated unfairly, but we cannot address that unfairness without taking into account the incentive structure of the industry and finding ways to align the interests of home care aides with those of the industry's powerful players.

Incentives and Pressures

The end goal is to enlarge the role of direct care workers and, by enabling them to play a broader role in the delivery of long-term services and supports, improve the quality of the jobs and the rewards that come with them. Budgetary pressures at both the federal and state levels militate against achieving this goal and of course, no insurance company is a charity and governments face constraints. These payers need to see change in the scope of practice of direct care workers and in their training and compensation as being in their interest, and they must also feel pressure to take action. How can this be achieved?

More Evidence   One element of the strategy is to nail the argument that in fact direct care workers whose jobs are expanded can make a real difference. I have presented a wide range of what I hope is convincing evidence to this effect, but what is missing is a credible, large-scale national demonstration. The power of evidence in this arena is shown by the impact of the one credible large-scale home care demonstration and evaluation—the Cash and Counseling demonstration initiated twenty years ago—in changing attitudes and showing that consumer-directed models are feasible and safe.

Recall that health care is a field in which the norm is to conduct large-scale demonstrations with carefully managed random assignment assessment. And recall that there is no national demonstration regarding how to improve long-term care and upgrade the role of home care aides. The lack of sustained and serious attention to improving home and community-based care stands in sharp contrast not only to the plethora of health care demonstration programs in general but also to the far more extensive research concerning quality in nursing homes. Although the lack of serious demonstrations is another symptom of the low status and lack of creativity in this arena, it need not remain this way, and launching a serious demonstration should be a priority.

Managed Care and Financial Incentives   I argued at length in the prior chapter that a managed care insurance company should have an interest in expanding the role of home care aides for two reasons: well-trained aides with a broader scope of practice can help prevent unnecessary medical expenses and keep people out of hospitals, and to the extent that work is shifted to lower-paid care workers, the insurance company saves money. This incentive holds for any version of managed care, but when Medicaid and Medicare are rolled into one program, the benefits grow because there are more potential savings and even stronger incentives to broaden the role of aides. I have shown that this version of managed care is slowly being rolled out across the country, and I have also provided examples of managed care models that broaden the scope of aides' work, such as the PACE program. That said, it is clear that managed care companies are not yet acting on these opportunities and that some public policy nudges are called for.

Governmental Pressure   Although it is tempting to throw up our hands and say that the states run Medicaid and hence national policy is not feasible, in fact this is not true. There are extensive federal regulations with respect to quality and standards in Medicaid in general and also with respect to standards in managed care. Indeed, these quality standards were updated as recently as 2016. Remarkably (but not surprisingly), they are silent with respect to home care aides. This should change: the money is public, and there is a very substantial public interest both in better care delivery and in improving opportunities for the low-wage workforce.

Concretely, managed care companies should be required to be creative with the role of each member of the care team, including home care aides, just as they are now required to report a wide range of quality measures and are penalized if they fall short. A softer version of this pressure would be to build in financial incentives for managed care companies that move in this direction. The idea would be to initiate a virtuous cycle in which the nature of the care delivery system begins to shift as companies, once pushed, see that they are achieving better results for less money.

Both federal and state authorities can use their purchasing power to shape working conditions and compensation and have done so in a variety of ways—for example, by requiring that contractors provide paid sick leave.[7] In the arena of health care, one example of the potential power of an engaged government comes from the effort to enact legislation permitting the new category "advanced aide" (see chapter 8). In that case, the political and legal logjam was finally broken when the Centers for Medicare and Medicaid Services used its funding power to insist on the adoption of modestly expanded scope of practice rules. The point again is that discretionary funds and regulations offer opportunities if policymakers are willing to take them up.

The logic laid out here applies just as strongly to states as to the federal government, and perhaps even more so, since it is at the state level that financial pressures are felt most intensely. As I have noted, long-term care puts tremendous pressure on state budgets. In a real sense, the states are in the same position as managed care insurance companies: they want to find cheaper ways to deliver services. For this reason, it should be in the interest of states to incentivize insurance companies to expand the role of aides as a way of reducing expenditures on both acute care and more expensive health care providers such as nurses and physical therapists. Of course, the states would have to be able to look beyond the short-term costs of improved compensation and training and see the long-term benefits.

Training   On the supply side, more extensive and effective training is essential. As I have noted at several points, the current way of training direct care workers is a hodgepodge.[8] Under federal regulations, home health home care aides must receive 75 hours of training, but this is clearly inadequate. Requirements in sixteen states exceed the federal requirement, but only six meet the Institute of Medicine's recommended 120 hours. The federal requirement for CNA training is also 75 hours; only thirty-one states have extended the training beyond this point. Training for the aides generally known as personal care assistants (but sometimes going by other titles) is left to the states, among which there is considerable variation, but only seven states require PCAs to meet the home health home care aide or CNA level of training. No state requires the level of training that is appropriate for the new set of responsibilities envisioned in this book.

Although several best practice training initiatives have shown the way forward (see chapter 7), any call for more training, as well as the broader vision for home care aides, will undoubtedly run up against opposition from some representatives of the disability community, who may view the effort as a step toward "medicalizing" long-term care and taking control out of the hands of consumers. As I hope I have made clear throughout the book, I am sympathetic to this perspective. It is fully understandable that a young and cognizant disabled person whose caregiver is a family member unlikely to make a career of the work would feel it inappropriate for the government to impose a set of requirements regarding the training of that caregiver. But this is not the dominant scenario, and it will become even less common as the population ages. One-third of consumer-directed home care aides are neither family members nor friends, and these aides are likely to stay in the field. Outside of consumer-directed care, the majority of home care aides are making a career of the work and a lack of training holds them back. How do we thread this needle? How do we remain respectful of the consumer-directed viewpoint while not allowing it to dominate and constrain opportunities for millions of others? This is a question that must be answered going forward.

Nothing prevents the federal government and state governments from setting training standards (currently there are no training standards at the federal level for Medicaid), and the training infrastructure is in place. Most states have community colleges with experience in training adult caregivers as well as nonprofits, which can also be effective along these lines. Public support for training in this high-growth, high-demand occupation is an appropriate use of human capital development resources.

Unpaid Family Caregivers

Any effort to improve our long-term care system must pay attention to the dominant role of family caregivers. As we have seen, nearly 21 million people provide unpaid care to family members or friends every year (see appendix B). And as we saw in chapter 3, the overwhelming majority of these caregivers receive no training and no direct support, nor are larger social policies supportive of them.

This reality has led to considerable conversation among advocates and efforts to improve the circumstances of family caregiving, and a number of reports and policy proposals have been produced.[9] It is worth noting, and lamenting, that the attention to the plight of family caregivers exceeds the attention given to paid home care aides. This difference in attention may be reasonable given the large numbers of family members involved in home care, but it may also reflect the fact that unpaid family caregivers are drawn from the entire social and demographic spectrum, whereas home care aides are more likely to be poor and minority, groups that have difficulty capturing public attention and sympathy. This complaint aside, it is unquestionably true that improving the circumstances of family caregivers is important.

The first step, and by far the most important one, is to strengthen our social safety net, a set of programs that is relevant to all people and not just to family caregivers. High on this list is paid family leave. As is well known, the United States lags the developed world in supporting family leave. The lack of paid family leave intensifies the difficulties confronting family caregivers as they juggle their work and their caregiving.

Offering family caregivers training opportunities to become more effective caregivers at home and convincing the medical establishment to include them in the care team are important steps. There are scattered demonstrations on each of these fronts, supported by a range of foundations as well as the AARP, and a few states are taking the lead. Nonetheless, the current level of commitment is patchy and incomplete.

MAKING IT ALL HAPPEN

Is it realistic to think that we can improve our system of long-term care by enabling people to stay at home and upgrading the role of home care aides? Certainly, the current political juncture, with its aversion to social programs and social spending, is not propitious. It also has to be acknowledged that the Affordable Care Act, though innovative in many important ways, only tinkered around the edges of improving our long-term care system. In effect, it kept us muddling through and reinforced our reliance on a poor, low-paid, trained workforce backstopped by an army of unpaid family members. But this said, there are some reasons to think that change is possible and some steps that can be taken to make it more likely.

I have stated and restated the first reason for optimism: the cold reality of demographics. The number of people who will need care is set to explode, and if present trends continue, the number of people willing to work as direct care workers (both paid aides and unpaid family members) will not keep up. I provide evidence on this point in chapter 9 and in appendix D. Leaving aside for the moment all concerns about the quality of care and about fairness, this demographic imperative should generate pressure to consider how to make direct care workers' jobs more attractive. That said, whether the population needing assistance can be mobilized is another question, and that is what I will focus on here.

At the core of a political strategy for change is uniting the power of consumers—the elderly and the disabled—with the power of organized direct care workers. A superficial reading might conclude that the interests of consumers and home care aides are in conflict because at least some consumers believe that low wages are in their interest. This conflict has in fact played out in the debates at the state level around training standards for consumer-directed caregivers and at the federal level with respect to the controversy over the minimum wage and overtime coverage. But we need to move beyond these narrowly framed disagreements and recognize that, more fundamentally, high-quality care is in everyone's interest.

To move in this direction, the disability community needs to be more flexible about training and compensation standards and less opposed to efforts to "medicalize" care by expanding the role of home care aides. For their part, the elderly and the advocacy and public policy community have to recognize the importance of continuity of care and consumer control with greater sensitivity than was displayed in the debates around the Fair Labor Standards Act.

If the consumer communities can come together, then the next step is to unite with producers—the advocates for home care aides. Here the union movement is important and can play a role at two levels. Health care unions that represent direct care workers should continue to push for more generous state Medicaid appropriations and higher compensation. Additionally, some of these unions—notably in Washington State and Massachusetts—have advocated for expanding the role of home care aides and are running training demonstration programs along these lines.

The challenge for unions is twofold. First, outside of New York, they are active mostly in states with consumer-directed programs, and while important, these programs represent an incomplete slice of the problem. Second, the recent *Harris v. Quinn* ruling, which undercut the public authority model through which unions established membership dues payments, has been a serious setback for unions (for more discussion, see chapter 9). Even if unions can overcome it, they will have to expend a great deal of energy on effectively organizing members that will be unavailable for other efforts.

In addition, unions and other forms of organized advocacy have a broader role to play. Recent years have seen a broad push for improved employment standards across the board—as exemplified in the "Fight For Fifteen" campaign, which has had an impact in a range of industries from retail to fast food to health care and pushed firms, governors, mayors, and city councils to upgrade standards. The broader role of unions and other advocates would be to link the potential energy of organized consumers with that of organized workers and push for changes that would benefit both.

Is this realistic? The Fight For Fifteen has been more successful than anyone would have predicted and has had a noticeable impact on national debates concerning fairness in the job market. But what political power would a coalition of consumers and home care aides have? A powerful example of what is possible is the evolution of the long-term care system in Oregon.

In the 1970s, Oregon's Project Independence was organized by a coalition of consumers—the Grey Panthers, the National Organization of Women, the National Council of Senior Citizens, and others—to push for a reorganization of the state's long-term care system away from nursing homes and toward home care and small living situations embedded in the community. This political movement succeeded not only in rebalancing the system in this direction but also in overcoming sustained opposition from nurses and rewriting nurse delegation legislation in just the direction advocated in this book. Today Oregon is seen as perhaps the most progressive state in the nation with respect to long-term care. The point here is that it is in fact possible to bring together diverse constituencies who share a common interest in improving long-term care and to weld these groups into an effective political force.

The Oregon effort addressed neither the working conditions nor the wages of home care aides, although later a strong union did emerge. Today's goal, in all states, would be to create strong coalitions advocating for improving long-term care, in part, by enlarging the jobs of home care aides and upgrading their compensation and working conditions in order to expand the supply of aides. The addition of a concern for aides adds to the potential political heft of such coalitions.

The potential support for change is there, but it also has to be understood that strong advocacy and political organizing is required and must come from both groups that are directly affected—both consumers and home care aides. Also needed is leadership from politicians; operating in their own self-interest, they must be made to see that this is an issue they can run with. There is certainly a strong and sizable constituency that would reward such leadership. A central attraction to political leadership should be that the issue of long-term care reform is powerful and broad-based, compelling to all income and demographic groups. In this sense, it is much like Social Security, a program that politicians across the political spectrum support and defend. The rewards for political leaders who take up the challenge of improving our long-term care system should be considerable, and it is reasonable to believe that this leadership could be forthcoming.

CONCLUSION

Enabling people to have lives that are as full and healthy and engaged as possible is without doubt among the most important goals of any society. When we are young and healthy, having such a life seems so simple that we give it no thought. When we are sick or frail or disabled, however, the challenges loom large. Tremendous effort has gone into helping the sick get better and improving their lives. The effort that has gone into achieving the same goal for the elderly and disabled is shamefully far below this standard.

This book has proposed ways in which we can move forward and take up the challenge of improving long-term care systems in this country. In rethinking how care is delivered, the health care system must recognize that direct care workers, both paid and unpaid, spend more time with clients than anyone else. The argument for improving these jobs is not simply based on equity or fairness or altruism. As this book has demonstrated, the reality is that better training, better compensation, and an expanded role will add up to both better care and reduced costs. The strategy I present here is one that not only improves the circumstances of consumers and workers but goes a long way toward paying for itself.

The coming explosion of demand, driven by demographics, will put these issues on the political map. The worst response would be to continue to muddle through, relying on a patchwork system composed of a poorly designed welfare system, expensive private insurance, burdensome out-of-pocket expenditures, and unpaid family labor. We certainly can do better. Approaching the issue realistically and pragmatically, we can align the incentives of medical providers and insurance companies so that better care is delivered more efficiently. We can recognize that families will always be the primary support for their loved ones and, without denying the role of personal responsibility, provide supports so that this care is not devastating. And we can also recognize that without an army of paid direct care workers who are empowered and trained and compensated decently, no system of long-term care can work well. This book has shown that all of these improvements are possible, but in the end it will require the mobilization of families and caregivers, the elderly and the disabled, to make it happen.

APPENDIX A: DEFINING THE EXTENT OF DISABILITIES

Estimating the extent of a person's disability can be complicated in several ways. One fundamental question is whether to utilize the tight definition based on criteria laid out in the Health Insurance Portability and Accountability Act (HIPPA) of 1996 or whether to use a more expansive definition based on self-reported difficulties and challenges. Second, if we use the more expansive definition (which I do for reasons laid out here), we must acknowledge that surveys differ in their coverage and measures of disability.

The HIPPA criteria for establishing a person's disability are having either (1) at least two ADLs (among eating, toileting, bathing, transferring, and continence) that last at least ninety days or (2) severe cognitive issues that require supervision. In broad strokes, these are the typical eligibility criteria for Medicaid and tax-qualified private insurance. The most recent estimate, utilizing a range of data and the Urban Institute's simulation model, is that 6.3 million people ages sixty-five and older were eligible for LTSS in 2015.[1] Other researchers using the same criteria but different data sources arrive at broadly similar conclusions.[2]

By comparison, the 2015 American Community Survey, taking a broader view, asked how many people ages sixty-five and older reported difficulties with self-care, independent living, ambulation, or cognition; it arrived at the figure of 13,923,663. In the discussion here, I utilize this broader conception because it is better aligned with the public policy issues and because the HIPPA definition is too restrictive when we consider that family caregivers help people with a broader range of disabilities.[3]

Other researchers have also focused on the broader view. The Kaiser Fam-

Table A.1   Disability Measures in the American Community Survey
and the Health and Retirement Survey

	American Community Survey, 2015	Health and Retirement Survey, 2012
Nature of survey	Nationally representative; includes people living in institutions	Nationally representative; includes only people ages fifty and older living at home
People ages fifteen and older: disability measures	*Cognitive:* serious difficulty concentrating, remembering, or making decisions *Ambulatory:* serious difficulty walking or climbing stairs *Self-care:* difficulty bathing or dressing *Independent living:* difficulty doing errands alone	*ADLs:* difficulty with walking, bathing, eating, preparing for bed, toileting, or dressing *IADLs:* difficulty with cooking, shopping, making phone calls, filling prescriptions, or handling money
People ages fourteen and younger: disability measures	*Hearing:* deaf or serious difficulty hearing *Vision:* blind or serious difficulty seeing even when wearing glasses	

Source: 2015 ACS and 2012 HRS.

ily Foundation employed the broader view in using the 2011 National Health and Aging Trends Survey to estimate the number of people living in the community with LTSS needs, and Vicki Freedman and Brenda Spillman used a similar strategy.[4] Both of these efforts arrive at a somewhat higher number than mine. On the other hand, the Institute of Medicine, utilizing data on Medicare recipients ages sixty-five and older, reported somewhat smaller numbers—namely, that in 2011, 10.9 million people received help with self-care or household activities or were in nursing homes.[5]

There are two last complications: surveys ask somewhat different questions about capacities and disabilities, and the definition of disability varies by age. It is not reasonable to ask whether a three-year-old can do errands on his or her own, yet this is an item on the list of issues for adults.

In table A.1, I describe the questions that are asked in the surveys I use.

Table A.2   Disabled People in the United States, by Age and
             Disability, 2015 American Community Survey

Age	Disability	Total
Ages zero to four	Hearing, vision	142,129 (0.7%)
Ages five to fourteen	Hearing, vision, self-care	945,313 (2.0)
Ages fifteen and older	See table A.1	31,647,082 (12.4)
Ages fifty and older	See table A.1	22,911,251 (20.6)
Ages sixty-five and older	See table A.1	13,923,663 (29.1)

Source: 2015 ACS.
Note: Figures include people who are institutionalized.

Table A.3   Disabled People in the United States, by Disability, 2012
             Health and Retirement Survey

	Any Disability	Two or More Disabilities
ADL	14,016,831 (15.4%)	7,434,042 (8.2%)
IADL	16,276,159 (17.9)	7,198,472 (7.9)
ADL or IADL	22,072,925 (24.3)	12,180,651 (13.4)

Source: 2012 HRS.

The ACS criteria for defining a person as disabled (which I use) are as follows:

Ages zero to four: hearing or vision difficulties

Ages five to fourteen: hearing, vision, or self-care difficulties

Ages fifteen and older: difficulties with self-care or independent living, difficulties with walking or climbing, or cognitive difficulties

Table A.2 shows the count of disabled persons.

As noted, the Health and Retirement Survey asks more concrete questions about ADLs and IADLs and does so for those ages fifty and older. Table A.3 reports the HRS results that can be compared to the ACS counts for ages fifty and older.

These data on disabilities are clearly central for understanding the demand for care and are used in Appendix D to estimate the future need for direct care workers.

APPENDIX B: COUNTING HOME CARE AIDES AND CERTIFIED NURSING ASSISTANTS

Counting CNAs is straightforward: virtually all of them work in nursing homes and there are clear definitions of their jobs in the census data. Counting home care aides is considerably more complicated.

Home care aides can be grouped into four categories: unpaid family caretakers, agency home care aides, self-employed home care aides who work "above the table," and self-employed home care aides who work in the "gray market" (they do not report their income to the IRS). There are also consumer-directed home care aides, who fall into either the agency or self-employed group.

All observers recognize these four categories, but our understanding of the size of each one is incomplete. The only national survey of home care aides ever executed by the federal government targeted only agency home care aides, and the Department of Labor, in its economic impact statement on extending the Fair Labor Standards Act to home care aides, simply gave up and declined to offer any estimate of the number of home care aides beyond agency and consumer-directed aides. However, it is very hard to understand the dynamics of the job market without some sense of the size of these groups because it is certainly the case that home care aides move between them.

An additional complication is that paid home care aides who work for agencies fall into two subgroups: home health aides, who are certified according to the Medicare rules and have a minimum of seventy-five hours of training, and personal care assistants, for whom there are some state but no federal certifications. For reasons laid out in the text, I have combined these two groups.

I proceeded as follows to come up with the estimates provided here:

- Using the American Community Survey, I estimated the number of all home care aides who work for pay "above the table."

- Again using the ACS, I then estimated the number of self-employed aides working for pay.

- Next, I estimated the number of consumer-directed home care aides, drawing on a national survey of programs.

- Finally, using the Health and Retirement Survey, I estimated the number of unpaid family caretakers (adjusted for the age limitations of the HRS).

THE NUMBER OF HOME CARE AIDES WORKING ABOVE THE TABLE

The American Community Survey asks people about their occupation and the industry in which they work and classifies the answers into standard three-digit census categories. Two occupational classifications capture home care aides: code 3600, which refers to "nursing, psychiatric, and home health aides," and code 4610, which refers to "personal care aides." I combined these two occupational groups. If the industry classification is "skilled nursing facilities" (8270) or "residential care facilities" (8290), I categorized the aides as certified nursing assistants. Home care aides are those employed in these industries: "employment services" (7580), "home health care services" (8170), "other health services" (8180), "individual and family services" (8370), "private household" (9290), and "administration of human resource programs" (9480). I ignored the small number of home care aides who are reported to be in industries that are clearly inappropriate.

For 2015, the resulting estimates are 2,199,893 home care aides and 1,288,819 CNAs.

There are two reasons why these are underestimates of the number of paid aides. First, there are people whose main job is in fact home care aide but who are unlikely to report to the census that they are working because they work under the table. These people work in the so-called gray market, whose size is unknown. Second, the count of home care aides working above the table is based on census occupational reports in which people identify their main job, but this does not capture people who work in a different main job (the one whose occupational title they report in the census) but also moonlight as home care aides and report their income from being an aide to the IRS (and hence are not in the gray market).

THE NUMBER OF SELF-EMPLOYED HOME CARE AIDES

Estimating the "1099 market" (those home care aides who are self-employed and work above the table) is potentially straightforward because the American Community Survey includes a question about whether the respondent is self-employed. One would think that this solves the problem of identifying those aides who are self-employed, and it certainly would for most jobs. However, many home care aides moonlight—that is, they work for an agency and also work on their own—in large part because agencies are often unable to provide them with as many hours as they want and need. Thus, my estimate of the size of the 1099 market is likely to be a lower bound.

In 2015, a total of 217,168 home care aides reported being self-employed, and these accounted for 9.8 percent of all home care aides. The fact that only 1.0 percent of CNAs reported themselves as self-employed adds credibility to this estimate. This estimate of the self-employed is probably a lower bound since some home care aides who work as regular employees for agencies (or are employed in a totally different line of work) no doubt also work on the side in a self-employed role.

One potential concern is confusion in the ACS over the status of consumer-directed home care aides, some of whom may inappropriately report themselves as self-employed although their paycheck comes from Medicaid via a state authority that handles payroll. This concern is substantially put to rest, however, by the fact that the rate of self-employment among home care aides in California is the same as it is for the nation as a whole, despite the fact that Medicaid-financed home care aides in California are entirely consumer-directed. This said, to the extent that such misreporting is a problem, this bias would lead me to overestimate the self-employed segment.

THE NUMBER OF CONSUMER-DIRECTED
HOME CARE AIDES

It is difficult to estimate the number of consumer-directed home care aides. It might seem natural to use the HRS data on family and friends who work for pay, but there is no way of knowing how many of them are paid via Medicaid (and hence are consumer-directed) and how many are paid out of pocket. (Friend or family caregivers are unlikely to be paid via insurance because insurance companies require that aides be certified.)

The best strategy is to start with the National Resource Center for Participant-Directed Services, which estimates that there are 838,000 clients in consumer-directed programs.[1] If there is just one home care aide per client, then this also represents the number of consumer-directed home care aides. However, home care aides (even consumer-directed ones) may work for more than one client. It is hard to arrive at a figure for the number of those who do, because family members working as home care aides would seem to be less likely than other home care aides to have more than one client. For this reason, it seems best to leave the 838,000 figure as is, understanding that it is an upper bound of the number of consumer-directed aides and that the real number may be 10 to 15 percent less.

THE NUMBER OF UNPAID FAMILY OR
FRIEND CAREGIVERS

As noted earlier, the Health and Retirement Survey asks questions about both paid and unpaid helpers and classifies them by relationship to the client: paid helper (presumably a home care aide), spouse, child, relative, or friend, neighbor, or stranger (called in the survey "individual"). I counted as unpaid family caregivers the spouses, children, relatives, and friends who are reported as not receiving pay. The "friend" category is the only ambiguous classification: in the HRS, it is termed "individual," and though I assumed that an "individual" might be a friend or neighbor, that might not be the case (and survey documentation does not clarify this point). The survey asks about up to eight helpers per client, and I aggregated all of these to arrive at a total number of unpaid helpers.

Because the HRS only refers to people ages fifty and older, I inflated the number of helpers by the ratio of total disabled to disabled who are ages fifty and older. I used the ACS to generate this ratio (which is 1.439).

According to these calculations, then, there are 20,659,915 unpaid family and friends caring for disabled people. Of these, 19,254,924 are spouses, children, or relatives.

APPENDIX C: TURNOVER AND COMMITMENT

The challenge in calculating the turnover of home care aides and CNAs moving in and out of the occupation (as opposed to moving to and from specific employers) is that no longitudinal surveys capture a large enough number of aides to produce reliable estimates. Adding to the problem is that the only available survey of home care aides, conducted by the federal government in 2007, was cross-sectional; moreover, it included only home care aides working for agencies (and hence excluded self-employed home care aides).

The solution to these challenges is to take advantage of the longitudinal possibilities of the Current Population Survey (CPS). The CPS is a cross-sectional survey, but the sampling design permits some limited longitudinal analysis. Because households and individuals are sampled for four months, ignored for eight months, and then resampled for another four months, it is possible to follow people if the households and individuals can be matched.

This well-known approach has been used for some time for one-year matches.[1] The problem, however, is that a substantial amount of classification error occurs over a one-year period when it comes to occupational change. That is to say, much of what might appear to be movement between occupations is simply due to the census mistakenly assigning different three-digit occupations to what in fact is the same job.

It turns out that a more accurate estimate of occupational change can be obtained by looking at month-to-month movements during the first four months that households and individuals are in the survey. During these four months, respondents are asked whether their occupation in, say, month 2 was the same as their occupation in month 1; if the answer is yes, then the month 1 occupation is simply copied into the response field. This eliminates misclassification.[2]

I matched individuals across each month by using a variable created by Minnesota Population Center researchers from the Integrated Public Use Microdata Series (IPUMS); this variable is based on a set of household and individual identification variables.[3] In addition to the IPUMs procedure, I also eliminated anyone whose sex or race changed from month to month or who was reported as being more than one year older on a month-to-month basis.

In the analysis that follows, I used the first four months for each individual and ignored the second four months in order to avoid having the same individual appear in the data more than once. The analysis is for the years 2010 to 2014—the recovery years after the Great Recession. The sample is limited to people ages eighteen or older and is further limited to people who worked during the first month in the four-month period.

I examined mobility by first looking at the rate at which respondents remained in the narrowly defined (see appendix B) occupation of home care aide (or CNA) between month 1 and month 4. I also looked more broadly at people who began in month 1 as a home care aide but remained in any health care occupation in month 4.[4] In calculating mobility rates out of the occupation, I also adjusted (as I explain later) for the fact that people who are more turnover-prone will leave in the first period and hence extrapolating turnover estimates into annual rates requires reducing the initial turnover rate by a percentage that I derive later.

Looking at the month 4 status of people who worked as home health home care aides in month 1, 77.6 percent continued as home care aides, 10.8 percent worked in another job, 3.3 percent were unemployed, and 8.0 percent were out of the labor force. If we broaden the "staying" category to include those who worked in any health care job, the rates are: 82 percent in health care, 6.5 percent in another job, 3.3 percent unemployed, and 8.0 percent out of the labor force.

As expected, turnover rates at the beginning of the four-month measurement period are higher because the turnover-prone left first. Looking at month-to-month retention in a home health home care aide job, the figure is 84 percent between months 1 and 2 and 90 percent between months 3 and 4. I adjusted the earlier reported four-month retention rate by increasing it by the ratio of months 3–4 to months 1–2, as just reported. Finally, I multiplied this adjusted four-month retention rate out twice to get a twelve-month turn-over rate of 32 percent for home care aides.

By contrast, 93.2 percent of registered nurses who were in that job in month 1 were still in the job in month 4; for physical therapists, the figure is 92.2 percent. If we look at other low-wage occupations, we see that the figure is 70.1 percent for food preparation workers and 78.6 percent for maids.

APPENDIX D: FUTURE SUPPLY AND DEMAND

Will the future supply of direct care workers match the need? To answer this question we must break it down into three specific questions: How many people will need help? Given this figure, how many direct care workers will be required? And what will be the supply of direct care workers?

The future demand for direct care workers will be driven by the future numbers of disabled. To estimate this figure I modified disability rates and demographic trends with assumptions about changes in the health status of the relevant demographic subgroups.

With respect to the need for direct care workers, we can look at today's "production function"—the ratio of direct care workers to the disabled. This ratio can be calculated for both direct care workers paid above the table and unpaid family caregivers. Applying this ratio to the future number of disabled gives us an estimate of how many paid direct care workers will be required as well as the number of unpaid family caregivers. This calculation assumes that other trends, notably technology, will not shift the production function. The implication of excluding gray market direct care workers (those paid below the table) from these calculations is discussed later in this appendix.

With respect to the supply of direct care workers, I began with the ratio of current direct care workers to the number of people in the current potential supply pool. I refer to this figure—the fraction of an age group working today as a direct care worker—as the "pull rate." I used the pull rate to calculate, based on the size of the future potential supply pool, the future supply of direct care workers—again assuming that nothing else changes. This calculation

Table D.1   Projected Demand for Long-Term Care, 2030 and 2040

Year	Population Age Sixty-Five and Older	Population Under Age Sixty-Five	Number of Disabled Age Sixty-Five and Older	Number of Disabled Under Age Sixty-Five	Total Disabled
2015	47,830,000	273,538,000	13,918,530	24,344,882	38,263,412
2030	74,107,000	285,295,000	21,565,137	25,391,255	47,003,348
2040	82,344,000	297,875,000	23,962,104	26,510,875	50,573,925

Source: Population projections taken from U.S. Census Bureau 2014, columns 3 and 4. Disability rates calculated from 2015 ACS (0.291 for ages sixty-five and older and 0.08 for ages zero to sixty-four).
Notes: To adjust the disability rate for ages sixty-five and older slightly upward, using the Urban Institute intermediate scenario, I added one-tenth of a percentage point per decade; this adjustment reflects the Urban Institute calculation that the increased weighting of the sixty-five-and-older group to older ages increases disability rates despite improvements in health status at each age.

assumed that the relative attractiveness of the job (relative to other competing occupations) will not be improved in a way that will attract more people to the work. (Improving the attractiveness of the work is, of course, a central theme of this book.) I engaged in a similar process for unpaid family caregivers.

I now turn to each of these steps.

THE DEMAND FOR CARE

As the first step in estimating demand, I used the 2015 ratio of the disabled to population groups, modified by assumptions about trends in health status, to project the number of disabled in 2030 and 2040. To keep things simple I worked with the ACS estimates of disability rates. (The rates in table D.1 are calculated from a weighted average of the rates for each of the age subgroups used in appendix A. I also adjusted for projected changes in health status, as described in the table note.)

THE PRODUCTION FUNCTION AND THE FUTURE DEMAND FOR DIRECT CARE WORKERS

To calculate how many direct care workers will be needed given the projections of the demand, I looked at the current ratio of direct care workers to disabled and then projected the future demand using this ratio.

There are 4,696,441 paid direct care workers (including both those paid above the table and those paid below the table) and 20,659,915 unpaid family members (see appendix B). (Note that in these calculations I included both home care aides and CNAs.) Thus, the ratio of paid direct care workers to disabled (the ACS-based production function rate) is 0.09, and the ratio of family and friend caregivers per disabled (the ACS-based production function rate) is 0.54.

The fact that paid and unpaid production function rates do not add up to 1.0 implies that on average a direct care worker works for more than one person. This is correct, as I have already discussed. In addition, note that the paid direct care worker figure is from the 2015 ACS while the unpaid family and friend caregiver figure is from the 2012 HRS.

Applying these production function ratios to the number of disabled in the year 2030, I estimated that the demand will be 4,285,586 for paid direct care workers and 25,378,948 for unpaid family and friend caregivers. For 2040, I estimated that the demand will be 4,611,137 for paid direct care workers and 33,801,180 for unpaid family and friend caregivers.

These increased demand numbers are less than the numbers estimated in some of the literature because I looked at the increase in demand by examining the increase in all disabled people rather than just the increase in the elderly. The number of younger disabled will not accelerate at the same rate as the number of elderly and so tamps down the overall increase.

THE SUPPLY OF DIRECT CARE WORKERS

For paid direct care workers, I looked at women, because very few of these workers are men. For unpaid family and friends who provide care, I looked at both men and women. Turning first to paid direct care workers (see table D.2), I undertook the analysis within age groups because the pull rate varies by age and the shift in demographics is age-related.

Age Group	Pull Rate
Eighteen to twenty-four	0.055
Twenty-five to thirty-four	0.032

Thirty-five to forty-four	0.030
Forty-five to sixty-four	0.031
Sixty-five to seventy-nine	0.016

The implications of these data taken together are shown in table D.3.

The calculations reported in table D.3 imply a shortfall in 2030 of about 151,201 paid direct care workers. The shortfall in 2040 would be about 355,301. However, these are considerable underestimates because, as we will see, the projected shortfall of family caregivers will substantially increase the demand for direct care workers.

The logic is the same with respect to unpaid family and friend caregivers, with one exception: we cannot utilize age-specific pull rates because we lack

Table D.2   Potential Supply of Paid Direct Care Workers, 2030 and 2040

Number of Women	Population in 2015	Number of Paid Direct Care Workers in 2015	Population in 2030	Population in 2040
Ages eighteen to twenty-four	8,196,000	454,016	15,047,000	15,083,000
Ages twenty-five to thirty-four	21,779,000	718,819	23,021,000	23,322,000
Ages thirty-five to forty-four	20,319,000	615,070	23,928,000	24,111,000
Ages forty-five to sixty-four	43,021,000	1,374,217	41,826,000	45,543,000
Ages sixty-five to seventy-nine	19,187,000	317,786	29,057,000	28,167,000

Source: U.S. Census Bureau 2014; 2015 ACS.

Table D.3   Projected Supply of Paid Direct Care Workers, 2030 and 2040

Age Group	2030	2040
Eighteen to twenty-four	833,608	835,602
Twenty-five to thirty-four	759,156	769,082
Thirty-five to forty-four	724,316	729,856
Forty-five to sixty-four	1,336,045	1,454,777
Sixty-five and older	481,258	466,517
Total	4,134,385	4,255,836

Source: U.S. Census Bureau 2014; 2015 ACS.

Table D.4   Projected Supply and Demand for Friend and Family Caregivers, 2030 and 2040

	Number of Eighteen- to Sixty-Four-Year Old Men and Women, 2015	Number of Unpaid Family or Friend Caregivers, 2012[a]	Pull Rate	Supply Based on 2015 Pull Rate and Population	Demand[b]
2015	199,903,000	20,659,915	0.103	—	—
2030	209,022,000	—	—	21,602,360	25,378,948
2040	219,690,000	—	—	22,704,895	33,801,180

Source: U.S. Census Bureau 2014; 2015 ACS.
[a]See appendix A.
[b]As calculated in table D.1.

data on the ages of these caregivers. Instead, we simply estimate pull rates for the entire age range, reported in table D.4.

These calculations imply a shortfall of unpaid family and friend caregivers of 3,776,508 in 2030 and 11,096,205 in 2040. This estimate is consistent with the findings of other analysts who also point to substantial future shortages of family caregivers.[1] This large shortfall will substantially increase the demand for paid direct care workers.

There are several reasons why these calculations of shortfalls, for both paid and unpaid help, may be too conservative. First, the pull-rate methodology implicitly assumes that the 2015 demand is adequately filled and that shortfalls arise only if the equivalent ratios are not met going forward. To the extent that there are current shortages, future shortages will be worse than those projected here.

Second, when it comes to paid direct care workers, I ignore under-the-table, gray-market aides. The effect of this is ambiguous, since they enter into both sides of the equation. Including them would lead to an increase in the projected demand, since they would be included in the production function, but their inclusion would also increase the projected supply by increasing the pull rate. Using plausible estimates of the size of the gray-market workforce, my view is that by excluding them I have on balance underestimated future shortages.

Finally, the likely shortfall of paid direct care workers will be actually worse than estimated here because a substantial number will be family and friends (see appendix A); the demographics are worse for this group because the population drop is sharpest in the forty-five to sixty-four age range.

ADDITIONAL CONSIDERATIONS

Changes in family circumstances have an unclear impact on the availability of caregivers. Divorce and smaller families may reduce the future availability of spouse and adult child caregivers. Women's labor force participation has gone up but is now leveling off, so their presence in the workforce will not necessarily reduce their availability for family care, but that may happen if their rising earnings increase the opportunity costs of providing care. The geographical dispersion of families makes caregiving more difficult, but on the other hand, longer life expectancy for men increases spouse availability. In short, estimating the impact of changes in family structure is a guessing game. All this said, if the rate at which family members are willing to provide unpaid help declines, then the shortage of paid direct care workers will become even more acute.

Immigration trends can also make a difference. But given the uncertainty about the policy trajectory, predictions seem unwise.

APPENDIX E: METHODS

Four kinds of data underlie this book:

• The literature on long-term care
• Administrative data
• Interviews with actors in the field
• Nationally representative surveys

THE LITERATURE ON LONG-TERM CARE

There is an extensive literature on a range of topics relevant to long-term care (although the literature on home care aides, as the book points out, is much smaller). Several hundred notes make my use of this literature obvious.

ADMINISTRATIVE DATA

Federal agencies collect administrative data on financial and utilization topics relevant to long-term care. These data have been collected, organized, and published by several organizations, most notably Truven Health Analytics, the Kaiser Family Foundation, the Pew Charitable Trusts, and AARP. I have drawn data, and in some cases repackaged them, from the many useful tables produced by these organizations.

INTERVIEWS WITH ACTORS IN THE FIELD

I conducted nearly 120 interviews with a wide range of people involved in delivering long-term care, setting policy for long-term care, advocating, or engaged in research. These interviews were invaluable, for both the data they provided and the insights harvested from many insightful informants.

Interviewees were selected through what sociologists term a "snowball sample." I began with a few recommendations and in the course of the initial interviews asked for other suggestions. I guided this process in several ways. First, I made sure that I obtained interviews with actors from all the relevant categories in the system. Second, to the extent possible, I tried to avoid an "echo" effect by pushing my interviewees to suggest other potential interviewees who had a different point of view or different experiences than theirs. An important technique for accomplishing this was to ask for anecdotes illustrating the issues and then request the names of the people on the different sides of the question.

The following list provides data on the number of interviews I conducted with the different actors in the field. The majority of the interviews were taped and transcribed; for those that were not (for example, because the informant did not want the interview to be taped), I took careful notes.

Long-Term Care Actors	Number of Interviews
Academic researchers	3
Policy advocates and researchers	21
Unions (including union training programs)	11
Home care agencies and nursing homes	18
Foundations	7
Insurance companies	9
Federal officials	10
State and local officials	9
Geriatric care managers	3
Individual aides and CNAs	7
Focus groups with aides and CNAs (roughly ten individuals per group)	4
Nurses	3
Physicians and psychologists	6
Lawyers	3

NATIONALLY REPRESENTATIVE SURVEYS

I used four nationally representative surveys: the American Community Survey, the Current Population Survey, the Health and Retirement Survey, and the National Home Health Aide Survey. For each survey, I undertook original data analysis. Although I describe my methods and what I do with these surveys in the chapters and (in much greater detail) in the appendices, I provide a very brief summary here.

American Community Survey: The ACS is a very large-scale (3.5 million addresses) survey conducted every year by the Census Bureau. In addition to its large sample size—which enables, for example, analysis at the state level—another big advantage of the ACS is that it includes data on nursing home residents as well as people living in the community. The ACS data I use include information on demographic characteristics, disability status, occupation, compensation, hours worked, and location.

Current Population Survey: The CPS is a smaller survey conducted monthly by the Census Bureau. Its best known use is the calculation of the monthly unemployment rate. The survey includes people living in the community who are over the age of fourteen and not in the armed forces. I use the CPS to analyze turnover and mobility, as described in appendix C.

Health and Retirement Survey: The HRS is a longitudinal survey of a nationally representative sample of people ages fifty and older, both in the community and in nursing homes. Housed at the University of Michigan, it is supported by the National Institute on Aging and the Social Security Administration. The sample is periodically renewed. In addition to demographic and financial data, the survey collects extensive information on health status and a range of variables regarding how people receive assistance and from whom.

National Home Health Aide Survey: This survey was conducted in 2007 and is representative of home health aides who work for agencies (and hence are neither self-employed nor paid below the table). Given these limitations, as well as the age of the survey, I use it sparingly.

NOTES

PREFACE

1. Osterman and Shulman 2011.

CHAPTER 1: INTRODUCTION

1. These figures are rounded up from my estimates based on the 2015 American Community Survey (ACS). Appendix A contains an extensive discussion of the methodology behind these numbers as well as results from other surveys and from alternative definitions of disability.

2. I deliberately use the term "home care aide" to avoid having to elaborate on different job titles and their subtle distinctions. More will be said on this later in the chapter.

3. "Walk a Day in My Shoes 2008, with Senator Barack Obama and Homecare Worker Pauline Beck," SEIU, uploaded August 9, 2007, available at: https://www.youtube.com/watch?v=miUS7WnMgBw (accessed February 16, 2017).

4. There are two kinds of home care aides: home health aides and personal assistants. In chapters 2 and 3, I discuss the distinctions between the two occupations, but in fact they are of relatively little importance.

5. 2015 ACS.

6. National Academies of Sciences, Engineering, and Medicine 2016; AARP and National Alliance for Caregiving 2015.

7. Keenan 2010, 4; Associated Press and NORC Center for Public Affairs Research 2016.

8. *Olmstead v. L.C.* 527 U.S. 581 (1999).

9. There is a debate about whether opting for home and community services actually saves money. Although it is true that the average home care client costs considerably less than the average nursing home client, the concern is that the option of home care brings clients "out of the woodwork" to claim services, whereas if the only alternative were nursing homes, they would grin and bear

their circumstances and not apply for assistance. Another concern is that people receiving unpaid help from family members will seek funding if supported home and community-based care is available. The evidence on the woodwork effect is mixed, but on balance there does appear to be a mild impact.

It seems logical that there would be a woodwork effect to some extent, and on balance (though not without disagreement), the literature supports this conjecture. That said, the safest conclusion from the literature is that the effect is not great enough to offset the budgetary gains from rebalancing. Of course, from a social policy perspective, a potential woodwork effect is not necessarily a bad thing, since it implies that people who need assistance but would not otherwise receive it are obtaining help (Eiken, Burwell, and Sredl 2013; Kaye, LaPlante, and Harrington 2009; Kemper 1988; LaPlante 2013; Wiener, Anderson, and Brown 2009).

10. "On a percentage basis," according to the health reporter Tara Parker-Pope, "surgery on the wrong side or area of the body is considered rare. But nonetheless, it affects hundreds of people a year, and hundreds more cases likely go unreported." See Parker-Pope, "When Surgeons Cut the Wrong Body Part," *New York Times,* November 28, 2007.

11. See chapter 2, note 33.

12. Kocher and Sahni 2011, 1371.

CHAPTER 2: THE LANDSCAPE OF LONG-TERM CARE IN THE UNITED STATES

1. See appendix B for the derivation of these figures.

2. 2015 ACS.

3. See appendix A for the derivation of these figures.

4. Reaves and Musumeci 2015.

5. Reinhard et al. 2014, table A16.

6. The best-known online agency is Honor, located in California. It stands apart from the main California system of consumer-directed care and does not accept Medicaid, but it does pay aides somewhat above going rates. Online models are still in a nascent stage, and it is unclear how they will play out and what the implications are for home care aides. Unlike grocery deliveries or handymen or any of the other services typically offered by these new platforms, home care is intimate and personal. Arm's-length platforms may not address people's need for thoughtful assessments and high touch management. In addition, it is not clear that an online platform can be responsive to the many opportunities for unexpected events and emergencies. Finally, unlike other bricks-and-mortar industries that have been disrupted, facilities and inventory are not a large part of home care industry costs, and so there is less margin for online platforms to underprice agencies. All this said, the experience in other industries certainly suggests that online platforms could become important over time.

7.   It is difficult to measure the reach of the home care industry because home
     health services can be provided by firms whose main identity lies elsewhere.
     That said, the Economic Census for the two main census categories "home
     health care services" and "services for the elderly and persons with disabilities"
     (NAICS codes 624120 and 621610) reports 43,503 establishments in 2007
     and 56,021 in 2012 (U.S. Census Bureau, Economic Census of the United
     States, available at: https://factfinder.census.gov/faces/nav/jsf/pages/index.xhtml,
     accessed February 16, 2017).
8.   The number of establishments subject to federal tax grew from 29,275 to
     41,295; the number of nonprofit establishments grew from 14,228 in 2007 to
     14,726 in 2012.
9.   Diment 2015.
10. Home Care Pulse 2015, 23.
11. National Center for Participant-Directed Services 2014.
12. Kaiser Family Foundation 2014.
13. U.S. Department of Health and Human Services, Administration on Aging 2012.
14. Joshua Wiener, Wayne Anderson, and David Brown (2009) find evidence for a
     shift by nursing homes to more Medicare clients, but they fail to find strong
     evidence for the other explanations cited here.
15. Grabowski, Stevenson, and Cornell 2012.
16. Harrington, Carrillo, and Garfield 2015.
17. Ibid., 2.
18. Doyle, Graves, and Gruber 2015. Random assignment occurs because the pa-
     tients who are followed differ by assignment to an ambulance company follow-
     ing a health emergency and different ambulance companies utilize different
     hospitals. Since the patient is not choosing the hospital, the distribution of
     health emergencies is random.
19. O'Shaughnessy 2013, 1.
20. SCAN Foundation 2012.
21. Grabowski et al. 2015.
22. Freedman and Spillman 2014, S47.
23. Caffrey et al. 2012.
24. Reaves and Musumeci 2015. Other sources offer somewhat different figures,
     but the basic story is the same across all studies (see Howes 2014; SCAN Foun-
     dation 2013).
25. Reaves and Musumeci 2015; Doty and Shipley 2012.
26. Reaves and Musumeci 2015, 4.
27. Health and Retirement Survey, University of Michigan, available at: http://
     hrsonline.isr.umich.edu/ (accessed February 16, 2017).
28. For a more detailed description of eligibility, see the extensive exposition of
     programs and eligibility at Medicaid.gov, "Long-Term Services and Supports,"
     available at: http://www.medicaid.gov/medicaid-chip-program-information/by

-topics/long-term-services-and-supports/long-term-services-and-supports
.html (accessed February 16, 2017).

29. Eiken et al. 2014, 1.

30. Ng et al. 2015, 5.

31. Eiken et al. 2015, 3.

32. Nationally, 53 percent of adults ages twenty-one or older with at least one ADL
and with an income of 250 percent of the poverty line receive services from
Medicaid. This figure varies by state, with New York being among the more
generous (65.8 percent) and Georgia one of the stingier (47.1 percent) (Reinhard et al. 2014, exhibit A6). Of course, Medicaid makes a big difference. In
the 2012 Health and Retirement Survey, among people ages fifty and older
with two or more disabilities, 32.7 percent of those on Medicaid received paid
help compared to 14.6 percent of those not on Medicaid (and of course the
non-Medicaid recipients were richer).

33. The question of whether people with income and assets above the limits should
be able to access Medicaid support for long-term services and supports is controversial. In my view, there is evidence that points in both directions on this
question. That said, it is important to recall that out-of-pocket payments can
bankrupt a family. Affordable private long-term care insurance that delivers
reasonable benefits is not available. Relying entirely on unpaid family members
can be a terrible burden, and if the person needs a nursing home level of care,
it is not even feasible. For many people, and from the perspective of public
policy, reliance on Medicaid is not optimal, but it is the only decent choice
available. Of course, the downside is the further draining of an already under-
funded program for poor people. The conclusion to be drawn is that, as I argue
in this book, we need to fix the entire system.

Assessing the extent of middle-class access to Medicaid LTC requires evidence on spend-down, on asset transfers, on lifetime earnings, and on whether
Medicaid crowds out private long-term care insurance, as well as evidence from
the growing ranks of elder care lawyers.

Spend-down refers to using up resources to meet income and assets limits
and become eligible for Medicaid long-term care. The best, and most recent,
analysis does not observe the actual process of spend-down but instead uses
the HRS to study the transition from not being eligible for Medicaid to being
eligible. Wiener and his colleagues (2013) find that spend-down is common:
9.6 percent of the non-Medicaid population transitioned to being Medicaid-
eligible between 1996 and 2008. The people who spent down accounted for
64.2 percent of Medicaid beneficiaries. Of those people who spent down,
46.1 percent did not use any long-term care. People who transitioned to eligibility were, on average, considerably poorer to begin with than those who
did not spend down, less likely to be well educated (about 5 percent had a
college education compared to about 20 percent of those who did not spend

down), and more likely to be a member of a minority group. The clear implication is that people who are higher in the income distribution are not utilizing Medicaid.

Research on the lifetime earnings of people receiving Medicaid support, however, implies a different conclusion. Richard Johnson and Gordon Mermin (2008) recently examined the income and assets of Medicaid recipients in nursing homes. As would be expected, those on Medicaid were substantially poorer than other nursing home residents. However, when their earnings history was examined, a different story emerged: people whose lifetime earnings were well up in the distribution nonetheless received Medicaid support. This implies a different assessment than that of the spend-down research.

Medicaid eligibility depends in part on not exceeding asset limits. By contrast to the findings on lifetime earnings, research on asset transfers fairly consistently concludes that what assets transfers do take place are small, and also that people whose incomes are reasonably close to Medicaid limits tend to have few assets to begin with (Government Accountability Office 2007; O'Brien 2005; Waidmann and Liu 2006; Wiener et al. 2013).

Health care economists concerned with understanding insurance markets have studied whether the availability of Medicaid has led people to avoid buying private long-term care (LTC) insurance and to plan on using Medicaid instead should they need to. Their research question is whether take-up of LTC insurance is lower than it would be absent Medicaid, and one way to examine this question is to take advantage of variation across states in Medicaid eligibility rules. The literature on the economics of health care has generally not been brought to bear on the question of whether people ineligible for Medicaid should be able to find a way to access Medicaid support for long-term services and supports, but it is clearly relevant since, if crowd-out occurs, the implication is that middle-class and even wealthier people expect to be able to find their way onto Medicaid should they need support. The most widely cited study of crowd-out found that it is significant (Brown and Finkelstein 2011). This finding has been replicated in other studies (Wagner 2015), and related research finds that people high in the income distribution value Medicaid as insurance (De Nardi, French, and Jones 2016).

Finally, I interviewed lawyers who specialize in helping people obtain Medicaid support for long-term care. These lawyers practiced in the more generous states—New York, Massachusetts, and California. Certainly, it is more difficult to obtain Medicaid support elsewhere in the country, but the strategies available in these states are illustrative of what is possible. Moreover, these large states obviously account for a substantial fraction of the Medicaid population.

Medicaid mandates a five-year "look-back" period: that is, any asset transfers aimed at meeting eligibility standards are disqualified if they occurred sooner than five years before Medicaid support was claimed. The key point here is that if people start planning five years before they need assistance, extensive maneuvers are not difficult and, according to the lawyers I spoke with, not uncommon. Nevertheless, the details of the look-back period can be byzantine (hence the need for the elder lawyers). Income restrictions are not a problem for nursing homes, however, because people can simply spend their available income on care and then have Medicaid pick up the remainder. It works like a copay. Income limits are more binding with respect to home care, but easier to deal with if a spouse is present (as is also true for nursing homes). For both nursing homes and home care, a substantial amount of assets are protected in the form of homeownership, and techniques can be used to protect assets, such as establishing annuities in a spouse's name or exotic trusts.

The overall conclusion of elder lawyers is that there are workable strategies that enable people whose income and assets are nontrivially higher than the nominal Medicaid limits to obtain Medicaid support. The very existence—and growth—of this legal specialty is at least suggestive that there is truth to this view.

In summary, evidence on spend-down and asset transfer suggests that middle-class access to the system is limited, whereas evidence on lifetime earnings and private insurance crowd-out and the reports of the elder lawyers bar point toward access.

34. See U.S. Census Bureau, "What Is the American Community Survey?" available at: http://www.census.gov/programs-surveys/acs/about.html (accessed February 16, 2017).

35. See the Health and Retirement Survey website at: http://hrsonline.isr.umich.edu (accessed February 16, 2017).

CHAPTER 3: THE DIRECT CARE WORKFORCE

1. Boris and Klein 2012, 31.
2. Ibid., 31.
3. Parker et al. 2014.
4. The data reported in this section are taken from my analysis of the 2015 ACS.
5. In a regression (using the 2015 ACS) in which the dependent variable is the log of annual earnings and controls include age, immigrant status, gender, and an indicator for poor English-speaking ability, the rate of return on any college for home care aides is 0.09, while for all other employees it is 0.45. Both estimates are statistically significant.
6. Bureau of Labor Statistics 1997.
7. Howard and Adams 2010.
8. National Institute for Occupational Safety and Health 2010.
9. Hanson et al. 2015; Seavey and Marquand 2011.
10. These quotes are taken from Visiting Nurse Service of New York 2015 (emphasis in original).

11. Foner 1994, 85.
12. See Centers for Disease Control and Prevention, "National Nursing Assistant Survey," at: http://www.cdc.gov/nchs/nnhs/nursing_assistant_tables.htm (accessed February 16, 2017).
13. Bishop 2014, S46.
14. Centers for Disease Control and Prevention (CDC), National Center for Health Statistics (NCHS), "2004–2005 Nursing Assistant Tables," available at: http://www.cdc.gov/nchs/nnhs/nursing_assistant_tables.htm (accessed February 16, 2017).
15. PHI 2016, 20–22.
16. CDC, NCHS, "2004–2005 Nursing Assistant Tables."
17. Eaton 2000, 597.
18. Elliot et al. 2014.
19. Lopez 2014.
20. For a very useful case study of CHCA, see Inserra, Conway, and Rodat 2002.
21. See, for example, Bernhardt et al. 2009.
22. Leberstein, Tung, and Connolly 2015.
23. Ibid., 9.
24. Ibid., 16.

CHAPTER 4: THE JOB MARKET

1. Home Care Pulse 2015, 144.
2. Dawson 2016, 43.
3. To compare the annual earnings of home care aides with the earnings of competing occupations, the following shows the results of a regression (using data from the 2015 ACS) that controls for gender, age, education, English-speaking ability, and immigration status and in which the dependent variable is annual earnings.

CNA	+$4,262
Hospital aide	+$8,798
Maid	+$337
Food prep worker	–$2,524
Waitress	+$464

4. Wilhelm et al. 2015.
5. U.S. Department of Health and Human Services 2011.
6. Engberg et al. 2009; Kemper et al. 2010.
7. PHI 2015.
8. Visiting Nurse Service of New York 2015.
9. Feldman 1993.
10. Howes 2005.
11. Lynch et al. 2005, 9.

12. Centers for Medicare and Medicaid Services 2010, 3.
13. Bishop et al. 2008.

CHAPTER 5: FAMILY CAREGIVERS AND CONSUMER-DIRECTED PROGRAMS

1. AARP Public Policy Institute and National Alliance for Caregiving 2015; Council of Economic Advisers 2014; Institute of Medicine 2008.
2. Spillman et al. 2014, 10; National Academy of Sciences, Engineering, and Medicine 2016, 2–6.
3. Spillman et al. 2014, 10–13.
4. National Academy of Sciences, Engineering, and Medicine 2016, 2–7.
5. According to the Institute of Medicine (2008, 253), "There is strong evidence that informal caregivers have a profound effect on long-term care processes and outcomes. Engaging families in patient care has been shown to improve outcomes in dementia . . . and in schizophrenia care . . . and also to postpone institutionalization."
6. Reinhard, Levine, and Samis 2012, 24.
7. Norma Coe and her colleagues (2016) use the Cash and Counseling Demonstration of Consumer-Directed Programs. As I discuss later in this chapter, despite their assumption—and that of other researchers—Cash and Counseling was not a true random assignment demonstration. That said, these results are strongly suggestive.
8. National Academy of Sciences, Engineering, and Medicine 2016, 4.
9. National Alliance for Caregivers, Center for Long Term Care Research and Policy, MetLife Mature Market Institute 2011.
10. Van Houtven, Coe, and Skira 2013.
11. Institute of Medicine 2008, 258; National Academies of Sciences, Engineering, and Medicine 2016, 3–32.
12. National Resource Center for Participant-Directed Services 2014; Ng et al. 2015.
13. Reinhard et al. 2014, exhibit A10.
14. Legislative Analyst's Office 2012.
15. Gorman 2015a, 2015b. In the Cash and Counseling demonstration, relatives accounted for 70 percent of home care aides and friends for 20 percent.
16. JSI Research and Training Institute 2009, 13.
17. National Resource Center for Participant-Directed Services 2014.
18. Boris and Klein 2012, 107.
19. Kafka 2007.
20. Squillace 2002, 3.
21. National Resource Center for Participant-Directed Services 2014.
22. Ibid., 4.
23. Benjamin et al. 2008.
24. Banijamali, Hagopian, and Jacoby 2012.

25. JSI Research and Training 2010.
26. Howes 2005.
27. Boris and Klein 2012, 108.
28. Gorman 2015(a).
29. Gorman 2015(b).

CHAPTER 6: INTRODUCTION TO PART II

1. MacDuffie 1995.
2. For a discussion, see Kochan and Osterman 1994.
3. This formulation draws from Appelbaum, Gittell, and Leana 2009.
4. See, for example, Appelbaum et al. 2000; Batt 2002; Leana and Pil 2006.
5. Ton 2014.
6. Gittell 2009.

CHAPTER 7: DIRECT CARE WORKERS: OPPORTUNITIES AND EVIDENCE

1. American Hospital Association 2013.
2. Bodenheimer 2008.
3. Cunningham 2013.
4. I appreciate an outside reviewer pushing me to make this point.
5. Blue Cross Blue Shield Association 2011, 36.
6. Bennett et al. 2010.
7. Nelson et al. 2010.
8. Ibid., 965.
9. Levine et al. 2013, 2.
10. Emanuel 2014, 86.
11. For more discussion, see the Care Transitions Program at: http://caretransi tions.org/ (accessed February 16, 2017); see also Coleman and Berman 2010.
12. Levine et al. 2013. The evaluation was not random assignment but rather based on interviews with teams using the model. The authors write: "The results that factored into that judgment were of two distinct types. Asked, in evaluation interviews, to identify the most significant outcomes of their work in Round Two, many participants described measurable, specific project results. These included reduced 30-day hospital readmission rates (achieved by five teams); high rates of family caregiver identification; assessment of caregiver needs soon after admission; increased caregiver education, leading to greater caregiver knowledge and confidence; safer discharges achieved through more comprehensive discharge planning and education; increased prior notification of discharge; caregiver involvement in medication reconciliation and management; and (in two teams) an increase in advance care planning, use of advance directives, and . . . documentation for patients and families" (33).
13. Thorpe 2011.

14. Ibid., 3.
15. Feldman 1997, 1.
16. Lewin et al. 2010.
17. Kangovi et al. 2014.
18. Bovbjerg et al. 2013, 14.
19. Walraven et al. 2010.
20. Russell et al. 2011.
21. Castle and Engberg 2005.
22. Stone and Wiener 2001, 27.
23. Garson et al. 2012.
24. California Improvement Network 2013; Grand-Aides, "Grand-Aides USA Summary," available at: http://www.grand-aides.com/the-program/grand-aides -summary (accessed February 16, 2017).
25. Dean et al. 2016.
26. Russell and Kurowski 2015.
27. Russell, McLaughlin, and Andreopoulos 2014, 6.
28. St. John's Well Child and Family Center and United Long Term Care Workers, "St. John's Enhanced Home Care Pilot Program," available at, http://phi national.org/sites/phinational.org/files/research-report/stjohnsreport.pdf (accessed February 16, 2017).
29. California Long-Term Care Education Center 2016.
30. Elliot et al. 2014.
31. Bishop 2014.
32. Cohen et al. 2016.
33. See the ALS Residence Initiative website at: http://www.alsri.org (accessed February 16, 2017).
34. Shier et al. 2014.
35. Grabowski et al. 2014.
36. Kane et al. 2007.
37. Zimmerman et al. 2016.

CHAPTER 8: OBSTACLES TO CHANGE

1. Paradise 2015, 2.
2. Eiken et al. 2014, 4.
3. Furrow et al. 2000, 586.
4. Kaiser Family Foundation, "State Health Facts," available at: http://kff.org /medicaid/state-indicator/medicaid-to-medicare-fee-index/ (accessed February 16, 2017).
5. Pew Charitable Trusts 2014, 44.
6. Ibid., 11, 44, and 45.
7. Standard & Poor's 2015, 53.
8. Medicare Payment Advisory Commission 2015, table 9-9.

9. "A single office of a 'senior care' franchise, as they are called in the industry, requires an investment of approximately $66,000; it is not uncommon for top franchises to build annual revenue to $1 million with a gross margin of 30 to 40 percent. When compared to the slim margins and high average initial investment of $500,000 for food and retail franchises, senior care franchises are extremely attractive investments. As a consequence, there are now about 40 franchise companies compared to 6 just 10 years ago" (Howes 2014, 6).

10. Home Care Pulse 2015, 66.

11. Fugazy 2015, 42.

12. Ng et al. 2014. For example, while most states utilize the 300 percent of Supplemental Security Income (SSI) standard, 24 percent of those reporting waiver programs utilize 100 percent (11). In the HCBS waiver programs, "many states used a mixture of fixed expenditure caps, service provision and hourly caps, and geographic limits" (12).

13. In 1997, Robyn Stone (1997) identified the integration of long-term care and acute care as one of the central challenges of improving the system.

14. Starr 1982.

15. See, for example, Schleiter 2010.

16. Kane 1997, 36.

17. Institute of Medicine 2008, 166; Dower, Moore, and Langelier 2013.

18. Farnham et al. 2011; Reinhard 2015; Sikma and Young 2003.

19. Reinhard and Quinn 2004.

20. Gwendolyn Lancaster, testimony before the joint legislative public hearing on the 2013–2014 executive budget proposal, health/Medicaid, Albany, N.Y., January 2013.

21. *Long Island Care at Home, Ltd., et al., v. Evelyn Coke*, Oral Argument, April 16, 2007, 27–28, available at: http://www.supremecourt.gov/oral_arguments /argument_transcripts/06-593.pdf (accessed February 16, 2017).

22. Ibid.

23. National Employment Law Project 2012, 14.

24. State House News Service, "Disabled, Caregivers Rally Against Hours Cap," *New Boston Post*, September 21, 2016, available at: http://newbostonpost .com/2016/09/21/disabled-caregivers-rally-against-hours-cap/ (accessed February 16, 2017).

CHAPTER 9: FORCES FOR CHANGE

1. For a review of communications technologies relevant to family caregivers, see National Academies of Sciences, Engineering, and Medicine 2016, 5–29ff.

2. LeadingAge 2016.

3. The Cochrane Collaborative is an organization widely respected for its review of the medical evaluation literature and summaries of what we do and do not know. It recently summarized where we stand on home technology: it found no

studies showing the effectiveness of smart technologies in the home (Martin et al., 2008).

4. The number of states offering managed long-term care grew from eight in 2004 to sixteen in 2012 to twenty-six in 2014. During this period, the number of people enrolled in these programs increased from 105,000 to over 1.1 million (Burwell 2013b; Truven Health Analytics 2012). Managed long-term care as a fraction of all Medicaid LTSS expenditures grew from 4.3 percent in 2008 to 9.9 percent in 2013 (Eiken et al. 2015, 20). In some states, managed care is mandatory for all LTSS, while elsewhere enrollment is voluntary. There is considerable variation across states in the populations included, the scope of the provider networks, the formulas for capitation rates, and a myriad other details that, while tiresome on their face, are quite important in determining the quality of the programs (Saucier et al. 2012).

5. Duals represent just 15 percent of Medicare enrollment and 17 percent of Medicaid enrollment, yet they account for 38 and 29 percent of spending, respectively (Burwell 2013a).

6. As of June 2015, only 355,000 people were enrolled in the federal demonstration programs (Kaiser Family Foundation 2015).

7. California Health Care Foundation 2014.

8. National Council on Disability 2013.

9. Sciegaj et al. 2013.

10. New York Legal Assistance Group 2015.

11. Nina Bernstein, "Lives Upended by Disputed Cuts in Home-Health Care for Disabled Patients," *New York Times,* July 20, 2016.

12. Health Management Associates 2015, 12.

13. Voluntary departures from each of the plans is under 1 percent a year, and with respect to patient satisfaction, the plans receive an average Medicare star rating of 4.4, compared to a national average of 3.4 (Health Management Associates 2015, 15). In 2015, the overall Medicare star rating was 4.1, compared to a national average for Medicare Advantage plans (the purely Medicare capitated model) of 3.9, and these results were obtained even though the dual-patient population is more complex than the pure Medicare population (ibid., 19). Furthermore, the plans are focused on keeping people in their homes and avoiding nursing homes. The incentive structure of capitation payments reinforces this, and the nursing home admission rates of SCO participants are well below statewide averages. (The plans receive nursing home reimbursement rates only if the client has been in an institution for ninety days or more. In addition, after the client leaves a nursing home, the institution rate is paid for the next ninety days at home.) Evaluations of the other long-standing dual program, Minnesota's Senior Health Options, reach similar conclusions (Institute of Medicine 2008, 91).

A story told to me by the CEO of one of the SCOs, Senior Whole Health, illustrates these points. A patient in Fall River, Massachusetts, was the patriarch of a large Portuguese family. Every Saturday, there would be a large family gathering and he would eat a lot of salty food and drink a lot of alcohol. Two days later, he would end up in the ER with fluid buildup. His care team knew his circumstances well enough to understand that he would refuse to change his habits because he was playing out his role in the family. Instead, they were able to convince the family doctor to prescribe extra drugs on Saturday, before each feast, and the problem was solved.

14. For a review of the literature, albeit one that is negative on balance, see Ghosh, Orfield, and Schmitz 2014.

15. Grassroots 2015.

16. Sarah Varney, "Private Equity Pursues Profits in Keeping the Elderly at Home," *New York Times,* August 20, 2016.

17. The Collaborative is drawing from the well-regarded INTERACT model of care transitions, which has been shown to reduce hospital readmissions for nursing home patients.

18. Brown et al. 2015, 432.

19. Clark 2013/2014.

20. Boris and Klein 2012; Sparer 1996.

21. Long 2013, 19.

22. On the concerns expressed by union supporters, see Boris and Klein 2012, 200.

CHAPTER 10: MOVING FORWARD

1. The number of young doctors training in gerontology is declining, and geriatricians earn less than internists despite having additional training; see Katie Hafner, "A Hole in Health Care," *New York Times,* January 26, 2016; Marquand and York 2016.

2. Priyanka Diyal McCluskey and Taryn Luna, "Walk-in Clinics Force Medicine to Rethink," *Boston Globe,* August 7, 2015.

3. Steve Lohr, "IBM Adds Medical Images to Watson, Buying Merge Healthcare for $1 Billion," *New York Times,* August 6, 2015.

4. U.S. Department of Health and Human Services, Health Resources and Services Administration 2016.

5. Government Accountability Office 2016.

6. See chapter 2, note 33.

7. Noam Scheiber, "Paid Sick Leave for Federal Contractors Is Mandated by Labor Department," *New York Times,* September 29, 2016.

8. The data in this section are taken from PHI, "Training Requirements by State," available at: http://phinational.org/policy/issues/training-credentialing/training-requirements-state (accessed February 16, 2017).

9. See, for example, Levine 2012; National Academies of Sciences, Engineering, and Medicine 2016; Reinhard et al. 2015.

APPENDIX A: DEFINING THE EXTENT OF DISABILITIES

1. Favreault and Dey 2016, 3.
2. Drabek and Marton 2015.
3. A point also made by Favreault and Dey (2016).
4. Garfield et al. 2015; Freedman and Spillman 2014.
5. National Academy of Sciences, Engineering, and Medicine 2016, 2–4.

APPENDIX B: COUNTING HOME CARE AIDES AND CERTIFIED NURSING ASSISTANTS

1. National Resource Center for Participant-Directed Services 2014.

APPENDIX C: TURNOVER AND COMMITMENT

1. Madrian and Lefgren 2000.
2. This possibility was introduced to me by Ted Mouw, to whom I am grateful.
3. Drew, Flood, and Warren 2013.
4. This calculation includes all health occupations (codes 3000–3655 and 4610) and no industry restrictions.

APPENDIX D: FUTURE SUPPLY AND DEMAND

1. Redfoot, Feinberg, and Houser 2013.

REFERENCES

AARP Public Policy Institute and National Alliance for Caregiving (NAC). 2015. "Caregiving in the U.S." Washington, D.C.: AARP Public Policy Institute and NAC (June).

American Hospital Association (AHA). 2013. "Workforce Roles in a Redesigned Primary Care Model." Washington, D.C.: AHA (January). Available at: http://www.aha.org/content/13/13-0110-wf-primary-care.pdf (accessed February 16, 2017).

Appelbaum, Eileen, Thomas Bailey, Peter Berg, and Arne L. Kalleberg. 2000. *Manufacturing Advantage: Why High-Performance Work Systems Pay Off.* Ithaca, N.Y.: Cornell University Press/ILR Press.

Appelbaum, Eileen, Jody Hoffer Gittell, and Carrie Leana. 2009. "High Performance Work Practices and Economic Recovery." LERA Commons (November 23).

Associated Press. NORC Center for Public Affairs Research. 2016. "Long-Term Care in America: Expectations and Preferences for Care and Caregiving." Chicago: Associated Press and University of Chicago, NORC Center for Public Affairs Research (May). Available at: http://www.longtermcarepoll.org/PDFs/LTC%20 2016/AP-NORC%20Long%20Term%20Care_2016.pdf (accessed February 16, 2017).

Banijamali, Sahar, Amy Hagopian, and Dan Jacoby. 2012. "Why They Leave: Turnover Among Washington's Home Care Workers." Seattle, Wash.: SEIU Healthcare 775NW (February).

Batt, Rosemary. 2002. "Managing Customer Services: Human Resource Practices, Quit Rates, and Sales Growth." *Academy of Management Journal* 45(3): 587–98.

Benjamin, A. E., Ruth E. Matthias, Kathryn Kietzman, and Walter Furman. 2008. "Retention of Paid Related Caregivers: Who Stays and Who Leaves Home Care Careers?" *The Gerontologist* 48(special issue 1): 104–13.

Bennett, Heather, Eric Coleman, Carla Perry, and Thomas Bodenheimer. 2010. "Health Coaching for Patients with Chronic Illness." *Family Practice Management* 17(5, September–October): 24–29.

Bernhardt, Annette, Ruth Milkman, Nik Theodore, Douglas Heckathorn, Mirabai Auer, James DeFilippis, Ana Luz Gonzalez, Victor Narro, Jason Perelshteyn, Diana Polson, and Michael Spiller. 2009. "Broken Laws, Unprotected Workers: Violations of Employment and Labor Laws in America's Cities." New York: National Employment Law Project.

Bishop, Christine E. 2014. "High-Performance Workplace Practices in Nursing Homes: An Economic Perspective." *The Gerontologist* 54(suppl. 1): S46–52.

Bishop, Christine, Dana Beth Weinberg, Walter Leutz, Almas Dossa, Susan Pfefferle, and Rebekah Zincavage. 2008. "Nursing Assistants' Job Commitment: Effect of Nursing Home Organizational Factors and Impact on Resident Well-being." *The Gerontologist* 48(special issue): 36–45.

Blue Cross Blue Shield Association (BCBS). 2011. "Building Tomorrow's Health Care System: The Pathway to High-Quality, Affordable Care." Chicago: BCBS (October).

Bodenheimer, Thomas. 2008. "The Future of Primary Care." *New England Journal of Medicine* 359(20): 2086–89.

Boris, Eileen, and Jennifer Klein. 2012. *Caring in America: Home Health Workers in the Shadow of the Welfare State.* New York: Oxford University Press.

Bovbjerg, Randall, Lauren Eyster, Barbara Ormond, Theresa Anderson, and Elizabeth Richardson. 2013. "The Evolution, Expansion, and Effectiveness of Community Health Workers." Washington, D.C.: Urban Institute (December).

Brown, Jeffrey, and Amy Finkelstein. 2011. "Insuring Long-Term Care in the United States." *Journal of Economic Perspectives* 25(4, Fall): 119–42.

Brown, Patrick, Sandra L. Hudak, Susan D. Horn, Lauren W. Cohen, David Allen Reed, and Sheryl Zimmerman. 2015. "Workforce Characteristics, Perceptions, Stress, and Satisfaction Among Staff in Green House and Other Nursing Homes." *Health Services Research* (November): 418–32.

Bureau of Labor Statistics (BLS). 1997. "Injuries to Caregivers Working in Patients' Homes." *Issues in Labor Statistics* (February).

Burwell, Brian. 2013a. "Medicaid Changes: Decisions Affecting Your State's Budget." Presentation to New England Fiscal Leaders Meeting. Boston (February 22).

———. 2013b. "The Continuing Shift to MLTSS and Its Impact on LTSS Providers." Presentation to the Twenty-Sixth Annual National Academy for State Health Policy (NASHP) Conference. Seattle (October 18).

Caffrey, Christine, Manisha Sengupta, Eunice Park-Lee, Abigail Moss, Emily Roenoff, and Lauren Harris-Kojetin. 2012. "Residents Living in Residential Care Facilities: United States, 2010." Data Brief 91. Washington: U.S. Department of Health and Human Services, Centers for Disease Control and Prevention, National Center for Health Statistics (April).

California Health Care Foundation. 2014. "In Transition: Seniors and Persons with Disabilities Reflect on Their Move to Medi-Cal Managed Care." Oakland: California Health Care Foundation (April).

California Improvement Network. 2013. "Webinar: Improving Care Through Workforce Innovation." Oakland: California Health Care Foundation (March 27). Available at: http://www.chcf.org/events/2013/cin-webinar-03-27-2013 (accessed February 16, 2017).

California Long-Term Care Education Center. 2016. "Care Integration and Training of Homecare Workers: Impact Study." California Long-Term Care Education Center (May).

Castle, Nicholas G., and John Engberg. 2005. "Staff Turnover and Quality of Care in Nursing Homes." *Medical Care* 43(6, June): 616–26.

Centers for Medicaid and Medicare Services (CMS). Direct Support Worker Resource Center. 2010. "Recruitment and Retention of Direct Support Professionals in North Dakota: Analysis of 2010 NDACP Data." Washington: CMS (November).

Clark, Paul. 2013/2014. "The Status of Unions in the U.S. Health Care Industry." *Perspectives on Work* (Summer 2013/Winter 2014): 23–25.

Coe, Norma, Jing Guo, R. Tamara Konetzka, and Courtney Harold Van Houtven. 2016. "What Is the Marginal Benefit of Payment-Induced Family Care?" Working Paper 22249. Cambridge, Mass.: National Bureau of Economic Research.

Cohen, Lauren, Sheryl Zimmerman, David Reed, Patrick Brown, Barbara Bowers, Kimberly Nolet, Sandra Hudak, and Susan Horn. 2016. "The Green House Model of Nursing Home Design and Implementation." *Health Services Research* 51(1, part II, February).

Coleman, Eric, and Amy Berman. 2010. "Improving Care Transitions: A Key Component of Health Reform." HealthAffairs Blog, April 29. Available at: http://healthaffairs.org/blog/2010/04/29/improving-care-transitions-a-key-component-of-health-reform/ (accessed February 16, 2017).

Council of Economic Advisers. 2014. "Nine Facts About American Families and Work." Washington, D.C.: Council of Economic Advisers (June).

Cunningham, Rob. 2013. "Health Workforce Needs: Projections Complicated by Practice and Technology Changes." Issue Brief 851. Washington, D.C.: National Health Policy Forum (October 22).

Dawson, Steve. 2016. "The Direct Care Workforce: Raising the Floor on Job Quality." *Generations* 40(1, Spring): 38–46.

Dean, Katie M., Laura A. Hatfield, Anupam B. Jena, David Cristman, Michael Flair, Kylie Kator, Geoffrey Nudd, and David C. Grabowski. 2016. "Preliminary Data on a Care Coordination Program for Home Care Recipients." *Journal of the American Geriatrics Society* 64(9, September): 1900–1903.

De Nardi, Mariacristina, Eric French, and John Bailey Jones. 2016. "Medicaid Insurance in Old Age." *American Economic Review* 106(11, November): 3480–3520.

Diment, Dmitry. 2015. "Take Care: Healthcare Reform and Growth of the Elderly Population Will Boost Demand." *IBISWorld Industry Report* 62412(February).

Doty, Pamela, and Samuel Shipley. 2012. "Long-Term Care Insurance Research Brief."

Washington: U.S. Department of Health and Human Services, Office of the Assistant Secretary for Planning and Evaluation (June).

Dower, Catherine, Jean Moore, and Margaret Langelier. 2013. "It Is Time to Restructure Health Professions Scope of Practice Regulations to Remove Barriers to Care." *Health Affairs* 32(11): 1972–76.

Doyle, Joseph, John Graves, and Jonathan Gruber. 2015. "Uncovering Waste in U.S. Healthcare." Working Paper 21050. Cambridge, Mass.: National Bureau of Economic Research (March 25).

Drabek, John, and William Marton. 2015. "Measuring the Need for Long-Term Services and Support." Issue brief. Washington: U.S. Department of Health and Human Services, Office of the Assistant Secretary for Planning and Evaluation (July).

Drew, Julia Rivera, Sarah Flood, and John Robert Warren. 2013. "Making Full Use of the Longitudinal Design of the Current Population Survey: Methods for Linking Records Across 16 Months." Working Paper 2013-02. Minneapolis: University of Minnesota, Minnesota Population Center (April).

Eaton, Susan. 2000. "Beyond 'Unloving Care': Linking Human Resource Management and Patient Care Quality in Nursing Homes." *International Journal of Human Resource Management* 11(3, June): 591–616.

Eiken, Steve, Brian Burwell, and Kate Sredl. 2013. "An Examination of the Woodwork Effect Using National Medicaid Long-Term Services and Supports Data." *Journal of Aging and Social Policy* 25(2): 134–45.

Eiken, Steve, Kate Sredl, Lisa Gold, Jessica Kasten, Brian Burwell, and Paul Saucier. 2015. "Medicaid Expenditures for Long-Term Services and Supports in FY 2013." Washington, D.C.: Truven Health Analytics (June 30).

Eiken, Steve, Kate Sredl, Paul Saucier, and Brian Burwell. 2014. "How Many Medicaid Beneficiaries Receive Long-Term Services and Supports?" Washington: Centers for Medicare and Medicaid Services and Truven Health Analytics (October 17).

Elliot, Amy, Lauren W. Cohen, David Reed, Kimberly Nolet, and Sheryl Zimmerman. 2014. "A 'Recipe' for Culture Change? Findings from the THRIVE Survey of Culture Change Adopters." *The Gerontologist* 54(suppl. 1): S17–24.

Emanuel, Ezekiel. 2014. *Reinventing American Health Care: How the Affordable Care Act Will Improve Our Terribly Complex, Blatantly Unjust, Outrageously Expensive, Grossly Inefficient, Error Prone System.* New York: Public Affairs.

Engberg, John, Nicholas G. Castle, Sarah B. Hunter, Laura A. Steighner, and Elizabeth Maggio. 2009. "National Evaluation of the Demonstration to Improve the Recruitment and Retention of the Direct Service Community Workforce." Santa Monica, Calif.: RAND Corporation.

Farnham, Jennifer, Heather Young, Susan Reinhard, Nirvana Petlick, Thomas Reinhard, and Vanessa Santillan. 2011. "New Jersey Nurse Delegation Pilot Report." New Brunswick, N.J.: Rutgers University Center for State Health Policy (April).

Favreault, Melissa, and Judith Dey. 2016. "Long-Term Services and Supports for Older Americans: Risks and Financing." Issue brief. Washington: U.S. Department of Health and Human Services, Office of the Assistant Secretary for Planning and Evaluation (February).

Feldman, Penny. 1993. "Work Life Improvements for Home Care Workers: Impact and Feasibility." *The Gerontologist* 33(1): 47–54.

———. 1997. "Labor Market Issues in Home Care." In *Home-Based Care for a New Century,* edited by Daniel Fox and Carol Raphael. Malden, Mass.: Blackwell.

Foner, Nancy. 1994. *The Caregiving Dilemma: Work in an American Nursing Home.* Berkeley: University of California Press.

Freedman, Vicki, and Brenda Spillman. 2014. "The Residential Continuum from Home to Nursing Home: Size, Characteristics and Unmet Needs of Older Adults." *Journal of Gerontology, Series B Psychological* 69(7): S42–50.

Fugazy, Danielle. 2015. "Bringing Health Care Home." *Mergers and Acquisitions: The Dealermaker's Journal* (February): 41–42.

Furrow, Barry, Thomas L. Greaney, Sandra H. Johnson, Timothy Stoltzfus Jost, and Robert L. Schwartz. 2000. *Health Law,* 2nd ed. St. Paul, Minn.: West Group.

Garfield, Rachel, Katherine Young, MaryBeth Musumeci, Erica L. Reaves, and Judy Kasper. 2015. "Serving Low-Income Seniors Where They Live: Medicaid's Role in Providing Community-Based Long-Term Services and Supports." Menlo Park, Calif.: Kaiser Family Foundation, Kaiser Commission on Medicaid and the Uninsured (September).

Garson, Arthur, Donna Gree, Lisa Rodriguez, Richard Beech, and Christopher Nye. 2012. "A New Corps of Trained Grand-Homecare Aides Has the Potential to Extend Reach of Primary Care Workforce and Save Money." *Health Affairs* 3(5): 1016–21.

Ghosh, Arkadipta, Cara Orfield, and Robert Schmitz. 2014. "Evaluating PACE: A Review of the Literature." Prepared for Office of Disability, Aging, and Long-Term Care Policy, Office of the Assistant Secretary for Planning and Evaluation, U.S. Department of Health and Human Services. Princeton, N.J.: Mathematica Policy Research (January).

Gittell, Jody Hoffer. 2009. *High Performance Healthcare: Using the Power of Relationships to Achieve Quality, Efficiency, and Resilience.* New York: McGraw-Hill.

Gorman, Anna. 2015a. "As Caregiving Shifts to the Home, Scrutiny Is Lacking." *Kaiser Health News,* January 5.

———. 2015b. "Lots of Responsibility for In-Home Care Provider—But No Training Provided." *Kaiser Health News,* January 6.

Government Accountability Office (GAO). 2007. "Medicaid Long-Term Care: Few Transferred Assets Before Applying for Nursing Home Coverage; Impact of Deficit Reduction Act on Eligibility Is Uncertain." Washington: GAO (March). Available at: http://www.gao.gov/new.items/d07280.pdf (accessed February 16, 2017).

———. 2016. "Medicaid Personal Services, CMS Could Do More to Harmonize Requirements Across Programs." GAO-17-28. Washington: GAO (November).

Grabowski, David, Daryl Caudry, Katie Dean, and David Stevenson. 2015. "Integrated Payment and Delivery Models Offer Opportunities and Challenges for Residential Care Facilities." *Health Affairs* 34(10): 1650–56.

Grabowski, David, James O'Malley, Christopher Afendulis, Daryl Caudry, Amy Elliot, and Sheryl Zimmerman. 2014. "Culture Change and Nursing Home Quality of Care." *The Gerontologist* 54(51): S35–45.

Grabowski, David, David G. Stevenson, and Portia Y. Cornell. 2012. "Assisted Living Expansion and the Market for Nursing Home Care." *Health Services Research* 47(6, December): 2296–2315.

Grassroots. 2015. "President Signs PACE Innovation Act." LeadingAge, November 8. Available at: http://www.leadingage.org/grassroots/president-signs-pace-innovation-act (accessed February 16, 2017).

Hanson, Ginger C., Nancy A. Perrin, Helen Moss, Naima Laharnar, and Nancy Glass. 2015. "Workplace Violence Against Homecare Workers and Its Relationship with Workers' Health Outcomes: A Cross-sectional Study." *BMC Public Health* 15(11). Available at: http://bmcpublichealth.biomedcentral.com/articles/10.1186/s12889-014-1340-7 (accessed February 16, 2017).

Harrington, Charlene, Helen Carrillo, and Rachel Garfield. 2015. "Nursing Facilities, Staffing, Residents, and Facility Deficiencies, 2009–2014." Menlo Park, Calif.: Kaiser Family Foundation, Kaiser Commission on Medicaid and the Uninsured (August). Available at: https://kaiserfamilyfoundation.files.wordpress.com/2015/08/8761-nursing-facilities-staffing-residents-and-facility-deficiencies.pdf (accessed February 16, 2017).

Health Management Associates. 2015. "Value Assessment of the Senior Care Option Program." Presentation to the Massachusetts Association of Health Plans Fourteenth Annual Health Policy Conference. Boston (July 21).

Home Care Pulse. 2015. *Private Industry Benchmarking Study 2015.* Rexburg, Idaho: Home Care Pulse LLC.

Howard, Ninica, and Darrin Adams. 2010. "An Analysis of Injuries Among Home Health Care Workers Using the Washington State Workers' Compensation Claims Database." *Home Health Care Quarterly* 29(2, April): 55–74.

Howes, Candace. 2005. "Living Wages and Retention of Homecare Workers in San Francisco." *Industrial Relations* 44(1): 139–63.

———. 2014. "Raising Wages for Home Care Workers: Paths and Impediments." New London: Connecticut College (February 25).

Inserra, Anne, Maureen Conway, and John Rodat. 2002. "The Cooperative Home Care Associates: A Case Study of a Sectoral Employment Development Approach." Washington, D.C.: Aspen Institute, Economic Opportunities Program (February).

Institute of Medicine. 2008. *Retooling for an Aging America: Building the Health Care Workforce.* Washington, D.C.: National Academies Press.

Johnson, Richard, and Gordon B. T. Mermin. 2008. "Long-Term Care and Lifetime Earnings: Assessing the Potential to Pay." Washington, D.C.: Urban Institute.

JSI Research and Training Institute. 2009. "Consumers' Experience in Massachusetts Personal Attendant Program." Boston: JSI Research and Training (November).

———. 2010. "The Experience of Personal Care Attendants (PCA) in the Massachusetts PCA Program." Boston: JSI Research and Training (March).

Kafka, Bob. 2007. "Agency with Choice Model." *Memphis Center for Independent Living Journal* (October 12).

Kaiser Family Foundation. 2014. "Total Number of Residents in Certified Nursing Facilities." Available at: http://kff.org/other/state-indicator/number-of-nursing-facility-residents/ (accessed February 16, 2017).

Kaiser Family Foundation. Kaiser Commission on Medicaid and the Uninsured. 2015. "Health Plan Enrollment in the Capitated Financial Alignment Demonstrations for Dual Eligible Beneficiaries." Menlo Park, Calif.: Kaiser Family Foundation (August).

Kane, Rosalie. 1997. "Boundaries of Home Care." In *Home Based Care for a New Century,* edited by Daniel Fox and Carol Raphael. Malden, Mass." Blackwell.

Kane, Rosalie A., Terry Lum, Lois J. Cutler, Howard B. Degenholtz, and Tzy-Chyi Yu. 2007. "Resident Outcomes in Small-Group-Home Nursing Homes: A Longitudinal Evaluation of the Initial Green House Program." *Journal of the American Geriatrics Society* 55(6, June): 832–39.

Kangovi, Shreya, Nandita Mitra, David Grande, Mary L. White, Sharon McCollum, Jeffrey Sellman, Richard P. Shannon, and Judith A. Long. 2014. "Patient-Centered Community Health Worker Intervention to Improve Posthospital Outcomes: A Randomized Clinical Trial." *Journal of the American Medical Association: Internal Medicine* 174(4): 535–43. doi:10.1001/jamainternmed.2013.14327.

Kaye, H. Stephen, Mitchell P. LaPlante, and Charlene Harrington. 2009. "Do Noninstitutional Long-Term Care Services Reduce Medicaid Spending?" *Health Affairs* 28(1): 262–72.

Keenan, Teresa A. 2010. "Home and Community Preferences of the 45+ Population." Washington, D.C.: AARP (November). Available at: http://www.caregiving.org/wp-content/uploads/2015/05/2015_CaregivingintheUS_Final-Report-June-4_WEB.pdf (accessed February 16, 2017).

Kemper, Peter. 1988. "Overview of Findings: The Evaluation of the National Long-Term Care Demonstration." *Health Services Research* 23(1): 161–74.

Kemper, Peter, Diane Brannon, Brigitt Heier, Joseph Vasey, Monika Setia, Jungyoon Kim, and Amy Stott. 2010. "The Better Jobs Better Care Management Practice Change Initiatives: Implementation and Effects on Job Outcomes and Turnover." University Park: Pennsylvania State University Center for Health Care and Policy (September 7).

Kochan, Thomas, and Paul Osterman. 1994. *The Mutual Gains Enterprise.* Cambridge, Mass.: Harvard Business School Press.

Kocher, Robert, and Nikhil R. Sahni. 2011. "Rethinking Health Care Labor." *New England Journal of Medicine* 365(15, October 13): 1370–72.

LaPlante, Mitchell P. 2013. "The Woodwork Effect in Medicaid Long-Term Services and Supports." *Journal of Aging and Social Policy* 25(2): 161–80.

LeadingAge. 2016. "Technology's Strategic Role and Adoption Are on the Rise Among the Largest Nonprofit Providers." Press release, December 15.

Leana, Carrie, and Fritz Pil. 2006. "Social Capital and Organizational Performance: Evidence from Urban Public Schools." *Organization Science* 17(3): 353–66.

Leberstein, Sarah, Irene Tung, and Caitlin Connolly. 2015. "Upholding Labor Standards in Home Care: How to Build Employer Accountability into America's Fastest-Growing Jobs." New York: National Employment Law Project (December).

Legislative Analyst's Office (LAO). 2012. "In-Home Supportive Services: Background and Policy Considerations of Proposed Integration into Medi-Cal Managed Care." Sacramento, Calif.: LAO (March 27). Available at: http://www.lao.ca.gov/handouts/socservices/2012/IHSS_3_27_12.pdf (accessed February 16, 2017).

Levine, Carol. 2012. "Long-Term Care and Long-Term Family Caregivers: Outdated Assumptions, Future Opportunities." In *Universal Coverage of Long-Term Care in the United States: Can We Get There from Here?* edited by Douglas Wolf and Nancy Folbre. New York: Russell Sage Foundation.

Levine, Carol, Deborah Halper, Jennifer Rutberg, and David Gould. 2013. "Engaging Family Caregivers as Partners in Transitions." New York: United Hospital Fund.

Lewin, Simon, Susan Munabi-Babigumira, Claire Glenton, Karen Daniels, Xavier Bosch-Capblanch, Brian E van Wyk, Jan Odgaard-Jensen, Marit Johansen, Godwin N. Aja, Merrick Zwarenstein, and Inger B. Scheel. 2010. "Lay Health Workers in Primary and Community Health Care for Maternal and Child Health and the Management of Infectious Diseases 2 (Review)." London and Baltimore: The Cochrane Collaboration.

Long, George. 2013. "Differences Between Union and Nonunion Compensation, 2001–2011." *Monthly Labor Review* 136(4): 16–23.

Lopez, Steven. 2014. "Culture Change and Shit Work: Empowering and Overpowering the Frail Elderly in Long-Term Care." *American Behavioral Scientist* 58(3): 435–52.

Lynch, Robert, Jon Fortune, Clifford Mikesell, and Terry Walling. 2005. "Wyoming Demonstrates Major Improvements in Retention by Enhancing Wages and Training." *Ancor Links* (October): 9–10.

MacDuffie, John-Paul. 1995. "Human Resource Bundles and Manufacturing Performance: Organizational Logic and Flexible Production Systems in the World Auto Industry." *Industrial and Labor Relations Review* 48(2): 197–221.

Madrian, Brigitte C., and Lars John Lefgren. 2000. "An Approach to Longitudinally Matching Current Population Survey (CPS) Respondents." *Journal of Economic and Social Measurement* 26(1): 31–62.

Marquand, Abby, and Amy York. 2016. "Squaring to the Challenge: Who Will Be Tomorrow's Caregivers?" *Generations* 40(1, Spring): 10–17.

Martin, Suzanne, Greg Kelly, W. George Kernohan, Bernadette McCreight, and Christopher Nugen. 2008. "Smart Home Technologies for Health and Social Care Support." *Cochrane Database of Systematic Reviews* 4. doi:10.1002/14651858. CD006412.pub2.

Medicare Payment Advisory Commission. 2015. "Report to Congress: Medicare Payment Policy." Washington, D.C.: Medicare Payment Advisory Commission.

National Academies of Sciences, Engineering, and Medicine. Health and Medicine Division. 2016. *Families Caring for an Aging America.* Washington, D.C.: National Academies Press.

National Alliance for Caregivers, Center for Long Term Care Research and Policy, MetLife Mature Market Institute. 2011. "The MetLife Study of Caregiving Costs to Working Caregivers." Westport, Conn.: MetLife Mature Market Institute (June). Available at: https://www.metlife.com/assets/cao/mmi/publications/studies /2011/Caregiving-Costs-to-Working-Caregivers.pdf (accessed February 16, 2017).

National Center for Participant-Directed Services. 2014. "Facts and Figures: 2013 National Inventory Survey on Participant Directory." Boston: Boston College School of Social Work.

National Council on Disability (NCD). 2013. *Medicaid Managed Care for People with Disabilities: Policy and Implementation Considerations for State and Federal Policymakers.* Washington, D.C.: NCD (March 18). Available at: http://www.ncd .gov/publications/2013/20130315/ (accessed February 16, 2017).

National Employment Law Project. 2012. "Comments to Proposed Revisions to the Companionship Exemption Regulations" (letter). RIN 1235-AA05. New York: National Employment Law Project (March 21).

National Institute for Occupational Safety and Health (NIOSH). 2010. "NIOSH Hazard Review: Occupational Hazards in Home Healthcare." Publication 2010-125. Washington: U.S. Department of Health and Human Services, Centers for Disease Control and Prevention (January).

National Resource Center for Participant-Directed Services. 2014. *Facts and Figures: 2013 National Inventory Survey on Participant Direction.* Boston: Boston College.

Nelson, Karen, Maria Pitaro, Andrew Tzellas, and Audrey Lum. 2010. "Transforming the Rise of Medical Assistants in Chronic Disease Management." *Health Affairs* 29(5): 963–65.

New York Legal Assistance Group. 2015. "Managed Long Term Care: Observations from Consumer Viewpoint—MLTC Year 3, FIDA—Year 1." New York: New York Legal Assistance Group (May).

Ng, Terence, Charlene Harrington, MaryBeth Musumeci, and Erica Reeves. 2014.

"Medicaid Home and Community Based Services Programs: 2011 Update." Menlo Park, Calif.: Kaiser Family Foundation (December).

―――. 2015. "Medicaid Home and Community-Based Services Programs: 2012 Data Update." Menlo Park, Calif.: Kaiser Family Foundation (November). Available at: http://kff.org/report-section/medicaid-home-and-community-based-services -programs-2012-data-update-conclusion/ (accessed February 16, 2017).

O'Brien, Ellen. 2005. "Medicaid's Coverage of Nursing Home Costs: Asset Shelter for the Wealthy or Essential Safety Net?" Washington, D.C.: Georgetown University Long-Term Care Financing Project (May). Available at: http://ltc.georgetown .edu/pdfs/nursinghomecosts.pdf (accessed February 16, 2017).

O'Shaughnessy, Carol. 2013. "The Basics: Assisted Living: Facilities, Financing, and Oversight." Washington, D.C.: George Washington University, National Health Policy Forum (January 29).

Osterman, Paul, and Beth Shulman. 2011. *Good Jobs America: Making Work Better for Everyone.* New York: Russell Sage Foundation.

Paradise, Julia. 2015. "Medicaid Moving Forward." Issues brief. Menlo Park, Calif.: Kaiser Family Foundation (March).

Parker, Emil, Stephanie Zimmerman, Sally Rodriguez, and Teresa Lee. 2014. "Exploring Best Practices in Home Health Care: A Review of Available Evidence on Select Innovations." *Home Health Care Management and Practice* 26(1): 17–33.

Pew Charitable Trusts. 2014. "State Health Care Spending on Medicaid: A 50-State Study of Trends and Drivers of Cost." Philadelphia: Pew Charitable Trusts (July).

PHI. 2015. "Paying the Price: How Poverty Wages Undermine Homecare in America." New York: PHI (February).

―――. 2016. "Raising the Floor: Quality Nursing Home Care Depends on Quality Jobs." New York: PHI (April).

Reaves, Erica, and MaryBeth Musumeci. 2015. "Medicaid and Long-Term Services and Supports: A Primer." Menlo Park, Calif.: Kaiser Family Foundation (May).

Redfoot Dennis, Lynn Feinberg, and Ari Houser. 2013. "The Aging of the Baby Boom and the Growing Care Gap: A Look at Future Declines in the Availability of Family Caregivers." Washington, D.C.: AARP Public Policy Institute.

Reinhard, Susan. 2015. "Research Findings on Nurse Delegation." Paper presented to AARP Public Policy Institute. New Jersey (March 13).

Reinhard, Susan, Lynn Friss Feinberg, Rita Choula, and Ari Houser. 2015. "Valuing the Invaluable: 2015 Update." Washington, D.C.: AARP Public Policy Institute (July).

Reinhard, Susan, Enid Kassner, Ari Houser, Kathleen Ujvari, Robert Mollica, and Leslie Hendrickson. 2014. "Raising Expectations 2014: A State Scorecard on Long-Term Services and Supports for Older Adults, People with Physical Disabilities, and Family Caregivers." Washington, D.C.: AARP.

Reinhard, Susan, Carol Levine, and Sarah Samis. 2012. "Home Alone: Family Caregivers Providing Complex Chronic Care." Washington, D.C.: AARP and United Hospital Fund (October).

Reinhard, Susan, and Winifred V. Quinn. 2004. "Oregon's Nurse Practice Policies for Home and Community Living." New Brunswick, N.J.: Rutgers University Center for State Health Policy (December).

Russell, David, and Daniel Kurowski. 2015. "Evaluating a Collaborative Health Coaching Partnership for High-Risk Heart Failure Patients." New York: Visiting Nurse Service of New York, Center for Home Care Policy and Research (February).

Russell, David, Katherine McLaughlin, and Evie Andreopoulos. 2014. "An Evaluation of the VNSNY Rehabilitation Home Health Homecare Aide Pilot Program." New York: Visiting Nurse Service of New York, Center for Home Health Care Policy and Research (February).

Russell, David, Robert J. Rosati, Peri Rosenfeld, and Joan M. Marren. 2011. "Continuity in Home Health Care: Is Consistency in Nursing Personnel Associated with Better Patient Outcomes?" *Journal of Health Care Quality* 33(6, December): 33–39.

Saucier, Paul Jessica Kasten, Brian Burwell, and Lisa Gold. 2012. "The Growth of Managed Long-Term Services and Supports (MLTSS) Programs: A 2012 Update." Washington, D.C.: Truven Health Analytics (July).

SCAN Foundation. 2012. "Trends in the Residential Care Industry." Data Brief Series 32. Long Beach, Calif.: SCAN Foundation (October). Available at: http://www.thescanfoundation.org/trends-residential-care-industry (accessed February 16, 2017).

———. 2013. "Who Pays for Long-Term Care in the U.S.?" Long Beach, Calif.: SCAN Foundation (January). Available at: http://www.thescanfoundation.org/sites/default/files/who_pays_for_ltc_us_jan_2013_fs.pdf (accessed March 31, 2017).

Schleiter, Kristin. 2010. "Ophthalmologists, Optometrists, and Scope of Practice Concerns." *American Medical Association Journal of Ethics* (formerly *Virtual Mentor*) 12(12, December): 941–45.

Sciegaj, Mark, Suzanne Crisp, Casey DeLuca, and Kevin J. Mahoney. 2013. "Participant-Directed Services in Managed Long-Term Services and Supports Programs: A Five-State Comparison." Washington: U.S. Department of Health and Human Services, Assistant Secretary for Planning and Evaluation, Office of Disability, Aging and Long-Term Care Policy (August).

Seavey, Dorie, with Abby Marquand. 2011. "Caring in America: A Comprehensive Analysis of the Nation's Fastest-Growing Jobs: Home Health Homecare Aides and Personal Care Homecare Aides." New York: PHI (December).

Shier, Victoria, Dmitry Khodyakov, Lauren Cohen, Sheryl Zimmerman, and Debra Saliba. 2014. "What Does the Evidence Really Say About Culture Change in Nursing Homes?" *The Gerontologist* 54(S1): S6–S16.

Sikma, Suzanne K., and Heather M. Young. 2003. "Nurse Delegation in Washington State: A Case Study of Concurrent Policy Implementation and Evaluation." *Policy, Politics, and Nursing Practice* 4(1): 53–61.

Sparer, Michael. 1996. *Medicaid and the Limits of State Health Reform.* Philadelphia: Temple University Press.

Spillman, Brenda, Jennifer Wolff, Vicki Freedman, and Judith Kasper. 2014. "Informal Caregiving for Older Americans: An Analysis of the 2011 National Study of Caregiving." Washington: U.S. Department of Health and Human Services, Office of the Assistant Secretary for Planning and Evaluation, Office of Disability, Aging, and Long-Term Care Policy (April).

Squillace, Marie. 2002. "Independent Choices: National Symposium on Consumer-Directed Care and Self-Determination for the Elderly and Persons with Disabilities: Summary Report." Washington: U.S. Department of Health and Human Services, Administration on Aging, Office for Community-Based Services, National Family Caregiver Support Program (February 15).

Standard & Poor's. 2015. "Industry Surveys: Health Care Providers and Services." New York: Standard & Poor's (May).

Starr, Paul. 1982. *The Social Transformation of American Medicine: The Rise of a Sovereign Profession and the Making of a Vast Industry.* New York: Basic Books.

Stone, Robyn. 1997. "Integration of Home and Community Based Services." In *Home Based Care for a New Century,* edited by Daniel Fox and Carol Raphael. Malden, Mass.: Blackwell.

Stone, Robyn I., and Joshua M. Wiener. 2001. *Who Will Care for Us: Addressing the Long-Term Care Workforce Crisis.* Washington: U.S. Department of Health and Human Services, Office of the Assistant Secretary for Planning and Evaluation (May 1).

Thorpe, Kenneth. 2011. "Building Evidence-Based Interventions to Avert Disease and Reduce Health Care Spending." Atlanta: Emory University (November).

Ton, Zeynep. 2014. *The Good Jobs Strategy.* Boston: Houghton Mifflin Harcourt/ New Harvest.

Truven Health Analytics. 2012. "The Growth of Managed Long-Term Services and Supports (MLTSS) Programs: A 2012 Update." Presentation to the Twenty-Fifth Annual National Academy for State Health Policy (NASHP) Conference. Baltimore (October 15).

U.S. Census Bureau. 2014. "Table 9: Projections of the Population by Sex and Selected Age Groups for the United States: 2015–2060." Washington: U.S. Census Bureau (December).

U.S. Department of Health and Human Services (HHS). 2011. "Understanding Direct Care Workers: A Snapshot of Two of America's Most Important Jobs." Washington: HHS (March).

U.S. Department of Health and Human Services, Administration on Aging, Administration for Community Living. 2012. "A Profile of Older Americans." Washington: HHS. Available at: https://aoa.acl.gov/Aging_Statistics/Profile/2012/index .aspx (accessed February 16, 2017).

U.S. Department of Health and Human Services. Health Resources and Services Administration. 2016. "Personal and Home Care Aide State Training (PHCAST) Demonstration Program Evaluation." Washington: HHS.

Van Houtven, Courtney Harold, Norma Coe, and Meghan Skira. 2013. "The Effect of Informal Care on Wages." *Journal of Health Economics* 32(1): 240–52.

Visiting Nurse Service of New York (VNSNY). Center for Home Care Policy and Research. 2015. "Homecare Aide Workforce Initiative (HAWI)." New York: VNSNY (January 7).

Wagner, Kathryn. 2015. "Medicaid Expansions for the Working Age Disabled: Revisiting the Crowd-out of Private Health Insurance." *Journal of Health Economics* 40(March): 69–82.

Waidmann, Timothy, and Korbin Liu. 2006. "Asset Transfer and Nursing Home Use: Empirical Evidence and Policy Significance." Menlo Park, Calif.: Kaiser Family Foundation, Kaiser Commission on Medicaid and the Uninsured (April).

Walraven, Carl, Natalie Oake, Alison Jennings, and Alan J. Forster. 2010. "The Association Between Continuity of Care and Outcomes: A Systematic and Critical Review." *Journal of Evaluation in Clinical Practice* 16(5): 947–56.

Wiener, Joshua, Wayne L. Anderson, and David Brown. 2009. "Real Choice Systems Change Program: Why Are Nursing Home Utilization Rates Declining?" Research Triangle Park, N.C.: RTI International (August).

Wiener, Joshua, Wayne L. Anderson, Galina Khatutsky, Yevgeniya Kaganova, and Janet O'Keeffe. 2013. "Medicaid Spend-Down: New Estimates and Implications for Long-Term Services and Supports Financing Reform." Research Triangle Park, N.C.: RTI International.

Wilhelm, Jess, Natasha Bryant, Janet P. Sutton, and Robyn Stone. 2015. "Predictions of Job Satisfaction and Intent to Leave Among Home Health Workers: An Analysis of the National Home Health Aide Survey." Washington: U.S. Department of Health and Human Services, Office of the Assistant Secretary for Planning and Evaluation (January).

Zimmerman, Sheryl, Barbara J. Bowers, Lauren W. Cohen, David C. Grabowski, Susan D. Horn, and Peter Kemper. 2016. "New Evidence on the Green House Model of Nursing Home Care: Synthesis of Findings and Implications for Policy, Practice, and Research." *Health Services Research* 51(1, part II, February).

INDEX

Boldface numbers refer to figures and tables.